# WINE MAKING JOURNAL, SECOND EDITION

*for the homemade wine maker*

## TABLE OF CONTENTS

Author:       Adam T. Courtney
ISBN-13:      9781500752842
ISBN-10:      1500752843
Cover Photo:  Michael Giguere
Website:      WineMakingJournal.com
              Facebook.com/WineMakingJournal
Copyright:    2006-2014 Adam T. Courtney

**SPECIAL THANKS TO:** Rob Simonar, Michael Giguere, Rikki Pahlow, Manny, Derrick Casper, John Herbes, Julie Wessley, Jack Keller, House of Homebrew, and of course everyone who has tasted my wine (the good and the bad). This journal was made with no thanks to Justin Buehler, again.

# ABBREVIATIONS
## USED IN THIS BOOK

Alc. Tol. . . . . Alcohol Tolerance

C . . . . Celsius

F . . . . Fahrenheit

Lbs . . . . Pounds

SO2 . . . . Sulfur Dioxide

Spc. Grv. . . . . Specific Gravity

TA . . . . Tartaric Acid

Tbsp . . . . Tablespoon

tsp . . . . Teaspoon

## CELSIUS TO FAHRENHEIT  $F=(C*1.8)+32$

| C | F | C | F | C | F | C | F | C | F | C | F | C | F |
|---|---|---|---|---|---|---|---|---|---|---|---|---|---|
| -20.0 | -4.00 | 0.00 | 32.0 | 20.0 | 68.0 | 40.0 | 104.0 | 60.0 | 140.0 | 80.0 | 176.0 | 100.0 | 212.0 |
| -19.0 | -2.20 | 1.00 | 33.8 | 21.0 | 69.8 | 41.0 | 105.8 | 61.0 | 141.8 | 81.0 | 177.8 | 101.0 | 213.8 |
| -18.0 | -0.40 | 2.00 | 35.6 | 22.0 | 71.6 | 42.0 | 107.6 | 62.0 | 143.6 | 82.0 | 179.6 | 102.0 | 215.6 |
| -17.0 | 01.40 | 3.00 | 37.4 | 23.0 | 73.4 | 43.0 | 109.4 | 63.0 | 145.4 | 83.0 | 181.4 | 103.0 | 217.4 |
| -16.0 | 3.20 | 4.00 | 39.2 | 24.0 | 75.2 | 44.0 | 111.2 | 64.0 | 147.2 | 84.0 | 183.2 | 104.0 | 219.2 |
| -15.0 | 5.00 | 5.00 | 41.0 | 25.0 | 77.0 | 45.0 | 113.0 | 65.0 | 149.0 | 85.0 | 185.0 | 105.0 | 221.0 |
| -14.0 | 6.80 | 6.00 | 42.8 | 26.0 | 78.8 | 46.0 | 114.8 | 66.0 | 150.8 | 86.0 | 186.8 | 106.0 | 222.8 |
| -13.0 | 8.60 | 7.00 | 44.6 | 27.0 | 80.6 | 47.0 | 116.6 | 67.0 | 152.6 | 87.0 | 188.6 | 107.0 | 224.6 |
| -12.0 | 10.4 | 8.00 | 46.4 | 28.0 | 82.4 | 48.0 | 118.4 | 68.0 | 154.4 | 88.0 | 190.4 | 108.0 | 226.4 |
| -11.0 | 12.2 | 9.00 | 48.2 | 29.0 | 84.2 | 49.0 | 120.2 | 69.0 | 156.2 | 89.0 | 192.2 | 109.0 | 228.2 |
| -10.0 | 14.0 | 10.0 | 50.0 | 30.0 | 86.0 | 50.0 | 122.0 | 70.0 | 158.0 | 90.0 | 194.0 | 110.0 | 230.0 |
| -9.00 | 15.8 | 11.0 | 51.8 | 31.0 | 87.8 | 51.0 | 123.8 | 71.0 | 159.8 | 91.0 | 195.8 | 111.0 | 231.8 |
| -8.00 | 17.6 | 12.0 | 53.6 | 32.0 | 89.6 | 52.0 | 125.6 | 72.0 | 161.6 | 92.0 | 197.6 | 112.0 | 233.6 |
| -7.00 | 19.4 | 13.0 | 55.4 | 33.0 | 91.4 | 53.0 | 127.4 | 73.0 | 163.4 | 93.0 | 199.4 | 113.0 | 235.4 |
| -6.00 | 21.2 | 14.0 | 57.2 | 34.0 | 93.2 | 54.0 | 129.2 | 74.0 | 165.2 | 94.0 | 201.2 | 114.0 | 237.2 |
| -5.00 | 23.0 | 15.0 | 59.0 | 35.0 | 95.0 | 55.0 | 131.0 | 75.0 | 167.0 | 95.0 | 203.0 | 115.0 | 239.0 |
| -4.00 | 24.8 | 16.0 | 60.8 | 36.0 | 96.8 | 56.0 | 132.8 | 76.0 | 168.8 | 96.0 | 204.8 | 116.0 | 240.8 |
| -3.00 | 26.6 | 17.0 | 62.6 | 37.0 | 98.6 | 57.0 | 134.6 | 77.0 | 170.6 | 97.0 | 206.6 | 117.0 | 242.6 |
| -2.00 | 28.4 | 18.0 | 64.4 | 38.0 | 100.4 | 58.0 | 136.4 | 78.0 | 172.4 | 98.0 | 208.4 | 118.0 | 244.4 |
| -1.00 | 30.2 | 19.0 | 66.2 | 39.0 | 102.2 | 59.0 | 138.2 | 79.0 | 174.2 | 99.0 | 210.2 | 119.0 | 246.2 |

## FAHRENHEIT TO CELSIUS  $C=(F-32)/1.8$

| F | C | F | C | F | C | F | C | F | C | F | C | F | C | F | C |
|---|---|---|---|---|---|---|---|---|---|---|---|---|---|---|---|
| 0.00 | -17.8 | 26.0 | -3.33 | 52.0 | 11.1 | 78.0 | 25.6 | 104 | 40.0 | 130 | 54.4 | 156 | 68.9 | 182 | 83.3 |
| 1.00 | -17.2 | 27.0 | -2.78 | 53.0 | 11.7 | 79.0 | 26.1 | 105 | 40.6 | 131 | 55.0 | 157 | 69.4 | 183 | 83.9 |
| 2.00 | -16.7 | 28.0 | -2.22 | 54.0 | 12.2 | 80.0 | 26.7 | 106 | 41.1 | 132 | 55.6 | 158 | 70.0 | 184 | 84.4 |
| 3.00 | -16.1 | 29.0 | -1.67 | 55.0 | 12.8 | 81.0 | 27.2 | 107 | 41.7 | 133 | 56.1 | 159 | 70.6 | 185 | 85.0 |
| 4.00 | -15.6 | 30.0 | -1.11 | 56.0 | 13.3 | 82.0 | 27.8 | 108 | 42.2 | 134 | 56.7 | 160 | 71.1 | 186 | 85.6 |
| 5.00 | -15.0 | 31.0 | -0.556 | 57.0 | 13.9 | 83.0 | 28.3 | 109 | 42.8 | 135 | 57.2 | 161 | 71.7 | 187 | 86.1 |
| 6.00 | -14.4 | 32.0 | 0.00 | 58.0 | 14.4 | 84.0 | 28.9 | 110 | 43.3 | 136 | 57.8 | 162 | 72.2 | 188 | 86.7 |
| 7.00 | -13.9 | 33.0 | 0.556 | 59.0 | 15.0 | 85.0 | 29.4 | 111 | 43.9 | 137 | 58.3 | 163 | 72.8 | 189 | 87.2 |
| 8.00 | -13.3 | 34.0 | 1.11 | 60.0 | 15.6 | 86.0 | 30.0 | 112 | 44.4 | 138 | 58.9 | 164 | 73.3 | 190 | 87.8 |
| 9.00 | -12.8 | 35.0 | 1.67 | 61.0 | 16.1 | 87.0 | 30.6 | 113 | 45.0 | 139 | 59.4 | 165 | 73.9 | 191 | 88.3 |
| 10.0 | -12.2 | 36.0 | 2.22 | 62.0 | 16.7 | 88.0 | 31.1 | 114 | 45.6 | 140 | 60.0 | 166 | 74.4 | 192 | 88.9 |
| 11.0 | -11.7 | 37.0 | 2.78 | 63.0 | 17.2 | 89.0 | 31.7 | 115 | 46.1 | 141 | 60.6 | 167 | 75.0 | 193 | 89.4 |
| 12.0 | -11.1 | 38.0 | 3.33 | 64.0 | 17.8 | 90.0 | 32.2 | 116 | 46.7 | 142 | 61.1 | 168 | 75.6 | 194 | 90.0 |
| 13.0 | -10.6 | 39.0 | 3.89 | 65.0 | 18.3 | 91.0 | 32.8 | 117 | 47.2 | 143 | 61.7 | 169 | 76.1 | 195 | 90.6 |
| 14.0 | -10.0 | 40.0 | 4.44 | 66.0 | 18.9 | 92.0 | 33.3 | 118 | 47.8 | 144 | 62.2 | 170 | 76.7 | 196 | 91.1 |
| 15.0 | -9.44 | 41.0 | 5.00 | 67.0 | 19.4 | 93.0 | 33.9 | 119 | 48.3 | 145 | 62.8 | 171 | 77.2 | 197 | 91.7 |
| 16.0 | -8.89 | 42.0 | 5.56 | 68.0 | 20.0 | 94.0 | 34.4 | 120 | 48.9 | 146 | 63.3 | 172 | 77.8 | 198 | 92.2 |
| 17.0 | -8.33 | 43.0 | 6.11 | 69.0 | 20.6 | 95.0 | 35.0 | 121 | 49.4 | 147 | 63.9 | 173 | 78.3 | 199 | 92.8 |
| 18.0 | -7.78 | 44.0 | 6.67 | 70.0 | 21.1 | 96.0 | 35.6 | 122 | 50.0 | 148 | 64.4 | 174 | 78.9 | 200 | 93.3 |
| 19.0 | -7.22 | 45.0 | 7.22 | 71.0 | 21.7 | 97.0 | 36.1 | 123 | 50.6 | 149 | 65.0 | 175 | 79.4 | 201 | 93.9 |
| 20.0 | -6.67 | 46.0 | 7.78 | 72.0 | 22.2 | 98.0 | 36.7 | 124 | 51.1 | 150 | 65.6 | 176 | 80.0 | 202 | 94.4 |
| 21.0 | -6.11 | 47.0 | 8.33 | 73.0 | 22.8 | 99.0 | 37.2 | 125 | 51.7 | 151 | 66.1 | 177 | 80.6 | 203 | 95.0 |
| 22.0 | -5.56 | 48.0 | 8.89 | 74.0 | 23.3 | 100 | 37.8 | 126 | 52.2 | 152 | 66.7 | 178 | 81.1 | 204 | 95.6 |
| 23.0 | -5.00 | 49.0 | 9.44 | 75.0 | 23.9 | 101 | 38.3 | 127 | 52.8 | 153 | 67.2 | 179 | 81.7 | 205 | 96.1 |
| 24.0 | -4.44 | 50.0 | 10.0 | 76.0 | 24.4 | 102 | 38.9 | 128 | 53.3 | 154 | 67.8 | 180 | 82.2 | 206 | 96.7 |
| 25.0 | -3.89 | 51.0 | 10.6 | 77.0 | 25.0 | 103 | 39.4 | 129 | 53.9 | 155 | 68.3 | 181 | 82.8 | 207 | 97.2 |

# MEASUREMENT CONVERSIONS

1 TABLESPOON = 3 TEASPOONS
1 CUP = 16 TABLESPOONS = 48 TEASPOONS = 8 OUNCES
1 PINT = 2 CUPS = 16 FLUID OUNCES = 1 POUND
1 QUART = 4 CUPS = 2 PINTS = 32 FLUID OUNCES = 2 POUNDS

| tsp | Tbsp | Cup | Pint | Ounce | Pound | Quart | tsp | Tbsp | Cup | Pint | Ounce | Pound | Quart |
|-----|------|-----|------|-------|-------|-------|-----|------|-----|------|-------|-------|-------|
| 1 | | | | | | | 49 | | | | | | |
| 2 | | | | | | | 50 | | | | | | |
| 3 | 1 | | | | | | 51 | 17 | | | | | |
| 4 | | | | | | | 52 | | | | | | |
| 5 | | | | | | | 53 | | | | | | |
| 6 | 2 | 1/8 | | 1 | | | 54 | 18 | 1 1/8 | | 9 | | |
| 7 | | | | | | | 55 | | | | | | |
| 8 | | | | | | | 56 | | | | | | |
| 9 | 3 | | | | | | 57 | 19 | | | | | |
| 10 | | | | | | | 58 | | | | | | |
| 11 | | | | | | | 59 | | | | | | |
| 12 | 4 | 1/4 | 1/8 | 2 | 1/8 | 1/16 | 60 | 20 | 1 1/4 | 5/8 | 10 | 5/8 | 5/16 |
| 13 | | | | | | | 61 | | | | | | |
| 14 | | | | | | | 62 | | | | | | |
| 15 | 5 | | | | | | 63 | 21 | | | | | |
| 16 | | 1/3 | | | | | 64 | | 1 1/3 | 2/3 | | | |
| 17 | | | | | | | 65 | | | | | | |
| 18 | 6 | 3/8 | | 3 | | | 66 | 22 | 1 3/8 | | 11 | | |
| 19 | | | | | | | 67 | | | | | | |
| 20 | | | | | | | 68 | | | | | | |
| 21 | 7 | | | | | | 69 | 23 | | | | | |
| 22 | | | | | | | 70 | | | | | | |
| 23 | | | | | | | 71 | | | | | | |
| 24 | 8 | 1/2 | 1/4 | 4 | 1/4 | 1/8 | 72 | 24 | 1 1/2 | 3/4 | 12 | 3/4 | 3/8 |
| 25 | | | | | | | 73 | | | | | | |
| 26 | | | | | | | 74 | | | | | | |
| 27 | 9 | | | | | | 75 | 25 | | | | | |
| 28 | | | | | | | 76 | | | | | | |
| 29 | | | | | | | 77 | | | | | | |
| 30 | 10 | 5/8 | | 5 | | | 78 | 26 | 1 5/8 | | 13 | | |
| 31 | | | | | | | 79 | | | | | | |
| 32 | | 2/3 | 1/3 | | | | 80 | | 1 2/3 | | | | |
| 33 | 11 | | | | | | 81 | 27 | | | | | |
| 34 | | | | | | | 82 | | | | | | |
| 35 | | | | | | | 83 | | | | | | |
| 36 | 12 | 3/4 | | 6 | 3/8 | 3/16 | 84 | 28 | 1 3/4 | | 14 | 7/8 | 7/16 |
| 37 | | | | | | | 85 | | | | | | |
| 38 | | | | | | | 86 | | | | | | |
| 39 | 13 | | | | | | 87 | 29 | | | | | |
| 40 | | | | | | | 88 | | | | | | |
| 41 | | | | | | | 89 | | | | | | |
| 42 | 14 | 7/8 | | 7 | | | 90 | 30 | 1 7/8 | | 15 | | |
| 43 | | | | | | | 91 | | | | | | |
| 44 | | | | | | | 92 | | | | | | |
| 45 | 15 | | | | | | 93 | 31 | | | | | |
| 46 | | | | | | | 94 | | | | | | |
| 47 | | | | | | | 95 | | | | | | |
| 48 | 16 | 1 | 1/2 | 8 | 1/2 | 1/4 | 96 | 32 | 2 | 1 | 16 | 1 | 1/2 |

## HYDROMETER CONVERSION

| Specific Gravity | Bailing Brix | Potential Alcohol | Sugar Ounces Per Gallon |
|---|---|---|---|
| 1.000 | 0 | 0.0% | 0 |
| 1.004 | 1 | 0.6% | 1.4 |
| 1.008 | 2 | 1.1% | 2.8 |
| 1.012 | 3 | 1.7% | 4.3 |
| 1.016 | 4 | 2.2% | 5.7 |
| 1.019 | 5 | 2.6% | 6.8 |
| 1.023 | 6 | 3.2% | 8.2 |
| 1.027 | 7 | 3.7% | 9.6 |
| 1.031 | 8 | 4.3% | 11.0 |
| 1.035 | 9 | 4.8% | 12.4 |
| 1.039 | 10 | 5.4% | 13.9 |
| 1.043 | 11 | 5.9% | 15.3 |
| 1.047 | 12 | 6.5% | 16.7 |
| 1.050 | 13 | 6.9% | 17.8 |
| 1.054 | 14 | 7.4% | 19.2 |
| 1.058 | 15 | 8.0% | 20.6 |
| 1.062 | 16 | 8.6% | 22.0 |
| 1.066 | 17 | 9.1% | 23.5 |
| 1.070 | 18 | 9.7% | 24.9 |
| 1.074 | 19 | 10.2% | 26.3 |
| 1.078 | 20 | 10.8% | 27.7 |
| 1.081 | 21 | 11.2% | 28.8 |
| 1.085 | 22 | 11.7% | 30.2 |
| 1.089 | 23 | 12.3% | 31.6 |
| 1.093 | 24 | 12.8% | 33.1 |

## HYDROMETER TEMPERATURE CORRECTION

| F | C | Adjustment |
|---|---|---|
| 32 | 0 | Subtract 1.6 |
| 41 | 5 | Subtract 1.3 |
| 50 | 10 | Subtract 0.8 |
| 60 | 15.6 | Correct |
| 68 | 20 | Add 1.0 |
| 77 | 25 | Add 2.2 |
| 86 | 30 | Add 3.5 |
| 95 | 35 | Add 5.0 |
| 104 | 40 | Add 6.8 |
| 113 | 45 | Add 8.8 |
| 122 | 50 | Add 11.0 |
| 131 | 55 | Add 13.3 |
| 140 | 60 | Add 15.9 |

## BUNG SIZES

| Bung Size | Bottom Diameter | Top Diameter |
|---|---|---|
| 2 | 1.6 cm | 1.9 cm |
| 3 | 1.8 cm | 2.2 cm |
| 5.5 | 2.4 cm | 2.8 cm |
| 6 | 2.7 cm | 3.2 |
| 6.5 | 2.8 cm | 3.4 |
| 7 | 3 cm | 3.8 |
| 7.5 | 3.1 cm | 3.9 |
| 8 | 3.3 cm | 4.1 |
| 8.5 | 3.6 cm | 4.3 |
| 9.5 | 3.8 cm | 4.6 |
| 10 | 4.3 cm | 5 |
| 10.5 | 4.5 cm | 5.3 |
| 11 | 4.9 cm | 5.6 |
| 11.5 | 5 cm | 6.3 |

## WINE ADDITIVES
(Teaspoons Per Ounce)

| | | |
|---|---|---|
| Ascorbic Acid | 6 | Teaspoons |
| Acid Blend | 6 | Teaspoons |
| Calcium Carbonate | 12 | Teaspoons |
| Citric Acid | 6 | Teaspoons |
| Gelatin | 8 | Teaspoons |
| Malic Acid | 6 | Teaspoons |
| Polyclar | 27 | Teaspoons |
| Stabilizer | 8 | Teaspoons |
| Sugar | 6 | Teaspoons |
| Tannin | 12 | Teaspoons |
| Tartaric Acid | 6 | Teaspoons |
| Yeast Energizer | 9 | Teaspoons |
| Yeast Nutrient | 5 | Teaspoons |

# YEAST QUICK REFERENCE

| Brand | Yeast | Temp (F) | Alc. Tol. | Notes |
|-------|-------|----------|-----------|-------|
| Lalvin | ICV D-47 | 59-68 | 14% | _____ |
| Lalvin | RC 212 | 68-86 | 16% | _____ |
| Lalvin | 71B-1122 | 59-86 | 14% | _____ |
| Lalvin | ICV KIV-1116 | 50-95 | 18% | _____ |
| Lalvin | EC-1118 | 50-95 | 18% | _____ |
| Red Star | Pateur Red | 64-86 | 16% | _____ |
| Red Star | Montrachet | 58-86 | 13% | _____ |
| Red Star | Cote des Blancs | 64-86 | 12-14% | _____ |
| Red Star | Pasteur Champagne | 59-86 | 13-15% | _____ |
| Red Star | Premier Cuvee | 45-95 | 18% | _____ |
| Red Star | Flor Sherry | 59-86 | 18-20% | _____ |
| White Labs | WLP700 Flor Sherry | 70 | 16% | _____ |
| White Labs | WLP705 Sake | 70 | 16% | _____ |
| White Labs | WLP707 California Pinot Noir | 70 | 16% | _____ |
| White Labs | WLP709 Sake #9 | 62-68 | 15-16% | _____ |
| White Labs | WLP715 Champagne | 70-75 | 17% | _____ |
| White Labs | WLP718 Avize | 60-90 | 15% | _____ |
| White Labs | WLP720 Sweet Mead | 70-75 | 15% | _____ |
| White Labs | WLP727 Steinberg-Geisenheim | 50-90 | 14% | _____ |
| White Labs | WLP730 Chardonnay White | 50-90 | 14% | _____ |
| White Labs | WLP735 French White | 60-90 | 16% | _____ |
| White Labs | WLP740 Merlot Red | 60-90 | 18% | _____ |
| White Labs | WLP749 Assmanshausen | 50-90 | 16% | _____ |
| White Labs | WLP750 French Red | 60-90 | 17% | _____ |
| White Labs | WLP760 Cabernet Red | 60-90 | 16% | _____ |
| White Labs | WLP770 Suremain Burgandy | 60-90 | 16% | _____ |
| White Labs | WLP775 English Cider | 68-75 | Med-High | _____ |
| Wyeast | 4021 Dry White / Sparkling | 55-75 | 17% | _____ |
| Wyeast | 4028 Red | 55-90 | 14% | _____ |
| Wyeast | 4242 Fruity White | 55-75 | 12-13% | _____ |
| Wyeast | 4244 Italian Red | 55-75 | 14% | _____ |
| Wyeast | 4267 Summation Red | 60-90 | 14% | _____ |
| Wyeast | 4767 Dry / Fortified | 60-90 | 14% | _____ |
| Wyeast | 4783 Sweet White | 55-75 | 14% | _____ |
| Wyeast | 4946 Bold Red / High Alcohol | 60-85 | 18% | _____ |

# YOUR FAVORITE RECIPES

Ingredients:_____1-1/4 lbs granulated sugar_____

2 cans Welch's 100% frozen grape concentrate

2 tsp acid blend

1 tsp pectic enzyme

water to make 1 gallon

Name:___Welch's Frozen Grape Juice Wine___

Yeast:___Red Star Premier Curvee___

___or Lalvin EC-1118 wine yeast___

Directions:___Bring 1 quart water to boil and dissolve sugar in the water. Remove from heat and add frozen concentrate. Add additional water to make 1 gallon and pour into secondary. Add remaining ingredients EXCEPT yeast. Cover with napkin fastened with rubber band and set aside 12 hours. Add activated wine yeast and re-cover with napkin. When active fermentation slows down (about 5 days), fit airlock. When clear, rack, top up, and refit airlock. After additional 30 days, stabilize, sweeten if desired and rack into bottles.

Notes:___Jack Keller's adaptation of a friend's recipe.

Printed with permission from and extra special thanks to:

Jack Keller's "The Winemaking Home Page" at winemaking.jackkeller.net

Jack's website has been a useful resource for all of my home winemaking needs!

---

Ingredients:_____

_____

_____

_____

_____

Name:_____

Yeast:_____

_____

_____

_____

Directions:_____

_____

_____

_____

_____

_____

_____

Notes:_____

_____

_____

_____

_____

# YOUR FAVORITE RECIPES

Ingredients:_____    Name:_____
_____    Yeast:_____
_____    _____
_____    _____
_____    _____
_____    _____

Directions:_____
_____
_____
_____
_____
_____

Notes:_____
_____
_____
_____
_____

Ingredients:_____    Name:_____
_____    Yeast:_____
_____    _____
_____    _____
_____    _____
_____    _____

Directions:_____
_____
_____
_____
_____
_____

Notes:_____
_____
_____
_____
_____

# YOUR FAVORITE RECIPES

Ingredients:_____     Name:_____
_____                 Yeast:_____
_____                 _____
_____                 _____
_____                 _____
_____                 _____

Directions:_____
_____
_____
_____
_____
_____

Notes:_____
_____
_____
_____
_____

Ingredients:_____     Name:_____
_____                 Yeast:_____
_____                 _____
_____                 _____
_____                 _____
_____                 _____

Directions:_____
_____
_____
_____
_____
_____

Notes:_____
_____
_____
_____
_____

# YOUR FAVORITE RECIPES

Ingredients:_____

_____

_____

_____

_____

_____

Name:_____

Yeast:_____

_____

_____

_____

_____

Directions:_____

_____

_____

_____

_____

_____

Notes:_____

_____

_____

_____

_____

---

Ingredients:_____

_____

_____

_____

_____

_____

Name:_____

Yeast:_____

_____

_____

_____

_____

Directions:_____

_____

_____

_____

_____

_____

Notes:_____

_____

_____

_____

_____

# YOUR FAVORITE RECIPES

Ingredients:_____    Name:_____
_____    Yeast:_____
_____    _____
_____    _____
_____    _____
_____    _____

Directions:_____
_____
_____
_____
_____
_____
_____

Notes:_____
_____
_____
_____
_____

---

Ingredients:_____    Name:_____
_____    Yeast:_____
_____    _____
_____    _____
_____    _____
_____    _____

Directions:_____
_____
_____
_____
_____
_____
_____

Notes:_____
_____
_____
_____
_____

# YOUR FAVORITE RECIPES

Ingredients:_____     Name:_____

_____     Yeast:_____

_____     _____

_____     _____

_____     _____

_____     _____

Directions:_____

_____

_____

_____

_____

_____

Notes:_____

_____

_____

_____

_____


Ingredients:_____     Name:_____

_____     Yeast:_____

_____     _____

_____     _____

_____     _____

_____     _____

Directions:_____

_____

_____

_____

_____

_____

Notes:_____

_____

_____

_____

_____

# YOUR FAVORITE RECIPES

Ingredients:_____  Name:_____
_____  Yeast:_____
_____  _____
_____  _____
_____  _____
_____  _____

Directions:_____
_____
_____
_____
_____
_____

Notes:_____
_____
_____
_____
_____

Ingredients:_____  Name:_____
_____  Yeast:_____
_____  _____
_____  _____
_____  _____
_____  _____

Directions:_____
_____
_____
_____
_____
_____

Notes:_____
_____
_____
_____
_____

# YOUR FAVORITE RECIPES

Ingredients:_____ Name:_____

_____ Yeast:_____

_____ _____

_____ _____

_____ _____

_____ _____

Directions:_____

_____

_____

_____

_____

_____

Notes:_____

_____

_____

_____

_____

---

Ingredients:_____ Name:_____

_____ Yeast:_____

_____ _____

_____ _____

_____ _____

_____ _____

Directions:_____

_____

_____

_____

_____

_____

Notes:_____

_____

_____

_____

_____

# YOUR FAVORITE RECIPES

Ingredients:_____    Name:_____

_____    Yeast:_____

_____    _____

_____    _____

_____    _____

_____    _____

Directions:_____

_____

_____

_____

_____

_____

_____

Notes:_____

_____

_____

_____

_____

---

Ingredients:_____    Name:_____

_____    Yeast:_____

_____    _____

_____    _____

_____    _____

_____    _____

Directions:_____

_____

_____

_____

_____

_____

Notes:_____

_____

_____

_____

_____

# YOUR FAVORITE RECIPES

Ingredients:_____     Name:_____

_____     Yeast:_____

_____     _____

_____     _____

_____     _____

_____     _____

Directions:_____

_____

_____

_____

_____

_____

Notes:_____

_____

_____

_____

_____

Ingredients:_____     Name:_____

_____     Yeast:_____

_____     _____

_____     _____

_____     _____

_____     _____

Directions:_____

_____

_____

_____

_____

_____

Notes:_____

_____

_____

_____

_____

# YOUR FAVORITE RECIPES

Ingredients:_____ Name:_____
_____ Yeast:_____
_____ _____
_____ _____
_____ _____
_____ _____

Directions:_____
_____
_____
_____
_____
_____

Notes:_____
_____
_____
_____
_____

---

Ingredients:_____ Name:_____
_____ Yeast:_____
_____ _____
_____ _____
_____ _____
_____ _____

Directions:_____
_____
_____
_____
_____
_____

Notes:_____
_____
_____
_____
_____

# PRIMARY FERMENTATION

Date: _____ / _____ / _____     #_____

Name:_____

Ingredients:_____

Spc.Grv. Before Correction:_____

_____

Sugar Added:_____

_____

Spc.Grv. After Correction:_____

_____

pH Before Correction:_____

_____

pH After Correction:_____

_____

TA Before:_____

_____

TA Correction:_____

_____

TA After:_____

Yeast:_____

Gallons of Must:_____

Totas SO2:_____

Notes:_____

_____

_____

_____

# SECONDARY FERMENTATION

| Date | Racked | Spc.Grv. | pH | SO2 | Gallons | Additions |
|------|--------|----------|-----|-----|---------|-----------|
| __ / __ / __ | ☐ | _____ | _____ | _____ | _____ | _____ |

Notes:_____

| __ / __ / __ | ☐ | _____ | _____ | _____ | _____ | _____ |

Notes:_____

| __ / __ / __ | ☐ | _____ | _____ | _____ | _____ | _____ |

Notes:_____

| __ / __ / __ | ☐ | _____ | _____ | _____ | _____ | _____ |

Notes:_____

| __ / __ / __ | ☐ | _____ | _____ | _____ | _____ | _____ |

Notes:_____

| __ / __ / __ | ☐ | _____ | _____ | _____ | _____ | _____ |

Notes:_____

# BOTTLING: _____ / _____ / _____

Spc.Grv. Before Sweetening:_____

Sugar Added:_____

Final pH:_____

Final SO2:_____

Final TA:_____

# of Bottles:_____

% Alcohol By Volume:_____

Notes:_____

_____

_____

_____

_____

_____

_____

_____

_____

ATTACH
LABEL
HERE

# TASTING

Color:_____

Body / Flavor:_____

Finish:_____

Tasting Notes:_____

_____

_____

_____

_____

_____

_____

_____

# NOTES FOR NEXT TIME: _____

_____

_____

_____

_____

_____

_____

# PRIMARY FERMENTATION

Date: _____ / _____ / _____     #_____

Ingredients:_____

_____

_____

_____

_____

_____

_____

_____

Yeast:_____

Gallons of Must:_____

Notes:_____

_____

_____

_____

_____

Name:_____

Spc.Grv. Before Correction:_____

Sugar Added:_____

Spc.Grv. After Correction:_____

pH Before Correction:_____

pH After Correction:_____

TA Before:_____

TA Correction:_____

TA After:_____

Totas SO2:_____

# SECONDARY FERMENTATION

| Date | Racked | Spc.Grv. | pH | SO2 | Gallons | Additions |
|------|--------|----------|-----|-----|---------|-----------|
| __/__/__ | ☐ | _____ | _____ | _____ | _____ | _____ |

Notes:_____

_____

| __/__/__ | ☐ | _____ | _____ | _____ | _____ | _____ |

Notes:_____

_____

| __/__/__ | ☐ | _____ | _____ | _____ | _____ | _____ |

Notes:_____

_____

| __/__/__ | ☐ | _____ | _____ | _____ | _____ | _____ |

Notes:_____

_____

| __/__/__ | ☐ | _____ | _____ | _____ | _____ | _____ |

Notes:_____

_____

| __/__/__ | ☐ | _____ | _____ | _____ | _____ | _____ |

Notes:_____

_____

# BOTTLING: _____ / _____ / _____

Spc.Grv. Before Sweetening:_____

Sugar Added:_____

Final pH:_____

Final SO2:_____

Final TA:_____

# of Bottles:_____

% Alcohol By Volume:_____

Notes:_____
_____
_____
_____
_____
_____
_____
_____
_____
_____

ATTACH
LABEL
HERE

# TASTING

Color:_____

Body / Flavor:_____

Finish:_____

Tasting Notes:_____
_____
_____
_____
_____
_____
_____
_____
_____

# NOTES FOR NEXT TIME: _____
_____
_____
_____
_____
_____
_____

# PRIMARY FERMENTATION

Date: _____ / _____ / _____        #_____        Name:_____

Ingredients:_____        Spc.Grv. Before Correction:_____

_____        Sugar Added:_____

_____        Spc.Grv. After Correction:_____

_____        pH Before Correction:_____

_____        pH After Correction:_____

_____        TA Before:_____

_____        TA Correction:_____

Yeast:_____        TA After:_____

Gallons of Must:_____        Totas SO2:_____

Notes:_____

_____

_____

_____

_____

# SECONDARY FERMENTATION

| Date | Racked | Spc.Grv. | pH | SO2 | Gallons | Additions |
|------|--------|----------|-----|------|---------|-----------|
| __ / __ / __ | ☐ | _____ | _____ | _____ | _____ | _____ |

Notes:_____

_____

| __ / __ / __ | ☐ | _____ | _____ | _____ | _____ | _____ |

Notes:_____

_____

| __ / __ / __ | ☐ | _____ | _____ | _____ | _____ | _____ |

Notes:_____

_____

| __ / __ / __ | ☐ | _____ | _____ | _____ | _____ | _____ |

Notes:_____

_____

| __ / __ / __ | ☐ | _____ | _____ | _____ | _____ | _____ |

Notes:_____

_____

| __ / __ / __ | ☐ | _____ | _____ | _____ | _____ | _____ |

Notes:_____

_____

# BOTTLING: ____ / ____ / ____

Spc.Grv. Before Sweetening:_____

Sugar Added:_____

Final pH:_____

Final SO2:_____

Final TA:_____

# of Bottles:_____

% Alcohol By Volume:_____

Notes:_____

_____

_____

_____

_____

_____

_____

_____

ATTACH
LABEL
HERE

# TASTING

Color:_____

Body / Flavor:_____

Finish:_____

Tasting Notes:_____

_____

_____

_____

_____

_____

_____

_____

# NOTES FOR NEXT TIME: _____

_____

_____

_____

_____

_____

_____

# PRIMARY FERMENTATION

Date: _____ / _____ / _____     #_____

Ingredients:_____

_____

_____

_____

_____

_____

_____

Yeast:_____

Gallons of Must:_____

Notes:_____

_____

_____

_____

_____

Name:_____

Spc.Grv. Before Correction:_____

Sugar Added:_____

Spc.Grv. After Correction:_____

pH Before Correction:_____

pH After Correction:_____

TA Before:_____

TA Correction:_____

TA After:_____

Totas SO2:_____

# SECONDARY FERMENTATION

| Date | Racked | Spc.Grv. | pH | SO2 | Gallons | Additions |
|------|--------|----------|-----|-----|---------|-----------|
| __ / __ / __ | ☐ | _____ | _____ | _____ | _____ | _____ |

Notes:_____

_____

| __ / __ / __ | ☐ | _____ | _____ | _____ | _____ | _____ |

Notes:_____

_____

| __ / __ / __ | ☐ | _____ | _____ | _____ | _____ | _____ |

Notes:_____

_____

| __ / __ / __ | ☐ | _____ | _____ | _____ | _____ | _____ |

Notes:_____

_____

| __ / __ / __ | ☐ | _____ | _____ | _____ | _____ | _____ |

Notes:_____

_____

| __ / __ / __ | ☐ | _____ | _____ | _____ | _____ | _____ |

Notes:_____

_____

# BOTTLING: _____ / _____ / _____

Spc.Grv. Before Sweetening:_____

Sugar Added:_____

Final pH:_____

Final SO2:_____

Final TA:_____

# of Bottles:_____

% Alcohol By Volume:_____

Notes:_____

_____

_____

_____

_____

_____

_____

_____

_____

ATTACH
LABEL
HERE

# TASTING

Color:_____

Body / Flavor:_____

Finish:_____

Tasting Notes:_____

_____

_____

_____

_____

_____

_____

_____

# NOTES FOR NEXT TIME: _____

_____

_____

_____

_____

_____

_____

# PRIMARY FERMENTATION

Date: _____ / _____ / _____    #_____    Name:_____

Ingredients:_____    Spc.Grv. Before Correction:_____

_____    Sugar Added:_____

_____    Spc.Grv. After Correction:_____

_____    pH Before Correction:_____

_____    pH After Correction:_____

_____    TA Before:_____

_____    TA Correction:_____

Yeast:_____    TA After:_____

Gallons of Must:_____    Totas SO2:_____

Notes:_____

_____

_____

_____

# SECONDARY FERMENTATION

| Date | Racked | Spc.Grv. | pH | SO2 | Gallons | Additions |
|------|--------|----------|-----|-----|---------|-----------|
| __ / __ / __ | ☐ | _____ | _____ | _____ | _____ | _____ |

Notes:_____

_____

| __ / __ / __ | ☐ | _____ | _____ | _____ | _____ | _____ |

Notes:_____

_____

| __ / __ / __ | ☐ | _____ | _____ | _____ | _____ | _____ |

Notes:_____

_____

| __ / __ / __ | ☐ | _____ | _____ | _____ | _____ | _____ |

Notes:_____

_____

| __ / __ / __ | ☐ | _____ | _____ | _____ | _____ | _____ |

Notes:_____

_____

| __ / __ / __ | ☐ | _____ | _____ | _____ | _____ | _____ |

Notes:_____

_____

# BOTTLING: ____ / ____ / _____

Spc.Grv. Before Sweetening:_____

Sugar Added:_____

Final pH:_____

Final SO2:_____

Final TA:_____

# of Bottles:_____

% Alcohol By Volume:_____

Notes:_____

_____

_____

_____

_____

_____

_____

_____

_____

ATTACH
LABEL
HERE

# TASTING

Color:_____

Body / Flavor:_____

Finish:_____

Tasting Notes:_____

_____

_____

_____

_____

_____

_____

_____

# NOTES FOR NEXT TIME: _____

_____

_____

_____

_____

_____

_____

_____

# PRIMARY FERMENTATION

Date: _____ / _____ / _____     #_____

Ingredients:_____

_____

_____

_____

_____

_____

_____

Yeast:_____

Gallons of Must:_____

Name:_____

Spc.Grv. Before Correction:_____

Sugar Added:_____

Spc.Grv. After Correction:_____

pH Before Correction:_____

pH After Correction:_____

TA Before:_____

TA Correction:_____

TA After:_____

Totas SO2:_____

Notes:_____

_____

_____

_____

# SECONDARY FERMENTATION

| Date | Racked | Spc.Grv. | pH | SO2 | Gallons | Additions |
|------|--------|----------|-----|-----|---------|-----------|
| __ / __ / __ | ☐ | _____ | _____ | _____ | _____ | _____ |

Notes:_____

_____

| __ / __ / __ | ☐ | _____ | _____ | _____ | _____ | _____ |

Notes:_____

_____

| __ / __ / __ | ☐ | _____ | _____ | _____ | _____ | _____ |

Notes:_____

_____

| __ / __ / __ | ☐ | _____ | _____ | _____ | _____ | _____ |

Notes:_____

_____

| __ / __ / __ | ☐ | _____ | _____ | _____ | _____ | _____ |

Notes:_____

_____

| __ / __ / __ | ☐ | _____ | _____ | _____ | _____ | _____ |

Notes:_____

_____

# BOTTLING: _____ / _____ / _____

Spc.Grv. Before Sweetening:_____

Sugar Added:_____

Final pH:_____

Final SO2:_____

Final TA:_____

# of Bottles:_____

% Alcohol By Volume:_____

Notes:_____

_____

_____

_____

_____

_____

_____

_____

_____

ATTACH
LABEL
HERE

# TASTING

Color:_____

Body / Flavor:_____

Finish:_____

Tasting Notes:_____

_____

_____

_____

_____

_____

_____

_____

# NOTES FOR NEXT TIME: _____

_____

_____

_____

_____

_____

_____

_____

# PRIMARY FERMENTATION

Date: _____ / _____ / _____       #_____

Ingredients:_____

_____

_____

_____

_____

_____

_____

Yeast:_____

Gallons of Must:_____

Notes:_____

_____

_____

_____

_____

Name:_____

Spc.Grv. Before Correction:_____

Sugar Added:_____

Spc.Grv. After Correction:_____

pH Before Correction:_____

pH After Correction:_____

TA Before:_____

TA Correction:_____

TA After:_____

Totas SO2:_____

# SECONDARY FERMENTATION

| Date | Racked | Spc.Grv. | pH | SO2 | Gallons | Additions |
|------|--------|----------|-----|-----|---------|-----------|
| __ / __ / __ | ☐ | _____ | _____ | _____ | _____ | _____ |
| Notes:_____ | | | | | | |
| __ / __ / __ | ☐ | _____ | _____ | _____ | _____ | _____ |
| Notes:_____ | | | | | | |
| __ / __ / __ | ☐ | _____ | _____ | _____ | _____ | _____ |
| Notes:_____ | | | | | | |
| __ / __ / __ | ☐ | _____ | _____ | _____ | _____ | _____ |
| Notes:_____ | | | | | | |
| __ / __ / __ | ☐ | _____ | _____ | _____ | _____ | _____ |
| Notes:_____ | | | | | | |
| __ / __ / __ | ☐ | _____ | _____ | _____ | _____ | _____ |
| Notes:_____ | | | | | | |

# BOTTLING: _____ / _____ / _____

Spc.Grv. Before Sweetening:_____

Sugar Added:_____

Final pH:_____

Final SO2:_____

Final TA:_____

# of Bottles:_____

% Alcohol By Volume:_____

Notes:_____

_____

_____

_____

_____

_____

_____

_____

_____

ATTACH
LABEL
HERE

# TASTING

Color:_____

Body / Flavor:_____

Finish:_____

Tasting Notes:_____

_____

_____

_____

_____

_____

_____

_____

# NOTES FOR NEXT TIME: _____

_____

_____

_____

_____

_____

_____

# PRIMARY FERMENTATION

Date: _____ / _____ / _____     #_____     Name:_____

Ingredients:_____     Spc.Grv. Before Correction:_____

_____     Sugar Added:_____

_____     Spc.Grv. After Correction:_____

_____     pH Before Correction:_____

_____     pH After Correction:_____

_____     TA Before:_____

_____     TA Correction:_____

Yeast:_____     TA After:_____

Gallons of Must:_____     Totas SO2:_____

Notes:_____

_____

_____

_____

_____

# SECONDARY FERMENTATION

| Date | Racked | Spc.Grv. | pH | SO2 | Gallons | Additions |
|------|--------|----------|-----|-----|---------|-----------|
| __ / __ / __ | ☐ | _____ | _____ | _____ | _____ | _____ |

Notes:_____

_____

| __ / __ / __ | ☐ | _____ | _____ | _____ | _____ | _____ |

Notes:_____

_____

| __ / __ / __ | ☐ | _____ | _____ | _____ | _____ | _____ |

Notes:_____

_____

| __ / __ / __ | ☐ | _____ | _____ | _____ | _____ | _____ |

Notes:_____

_____

| __ / __ / __ | ☐ | _____ | _____ | _____ | _____ | _____ |

Notes:_____

_____

| __ / __ / __ | ☐ | _____ | _____ | _____ | _____ | _____ |

Notes:_____

_____

# BOTTLING: _____ / _____ / _____

Spc.Grv. Before Sweetening:_____

Sugar Added:_____

Final pH:_____

Final SO2:_____

Final TA:_____

# of Bottles:_____

% Alcohol By Volume:_____

Notes:_____

_____

_____

_____

_____

_____

_____

_____

_____

ATTACH
LABEL
HERE

# TASTING

Color:_____

Body / Flavor:_____

Finish:_____

Tasting Notes:_____

_____

_____

_____

_____

_____

_____

_____

# NOTES FOR NEXT TIME: _____

_____

_____

_____

_____

_____

_____

_____

# PRIMARY FERMENTATION

Date: _____ / _____ / _____     #_____     Name:_____

Ingredients:_____     Spc.Grv. Before Correction:_____

_____     Sugar Added:_____

_____     Spc.Grv. After Correction:_____

_____     pH Before Correction:_____

_____     pH After Correction:_____

_____     TA Before:_____

_____     TA Correction:_____

Yeast:_____     TA After:_____

Gallons of Must:_____     Totas SO2:_____

Notes:_____

_____

_____

_____

_____

# SECONDARY FERMENTATION

| Date | Racked | Spc.Grv. | pH | SO2 | Gallons | Additions |
|------|--------|----------|-----|-----|---------|-----------|
| __ / __ / __ | ☐ | _____ | _____ | _____ | _____ | _____ |

Notes:_____

_____

| __ / __ / __ | ☐ | _____ | _____ | _____ | _____ | _____ |

Notes:_____

_____

| __ / __ / __ | ☐ | _____ | _____ | _____ | _____ | _____ |

Notes:_____

_____

| __ / __ / __ | ☐ | _____ | _____ | _____ | _____ | _____ |

Notes:_____

_____

| __ / __ / __ | ☐ | _____ | _____ | _____ | _____ | _____ |

Notes:_____

_____

| __ / __ / __ | ☐ | _____ | _____ | _____ | _____ | _____ |

Notes:_____

_____

# BOTTLING: _____ / _____ / _____

Spc.Grv. Before Sweetening:_____

Sugar Added:_____

Final pH:_____

Final SO2:_____

Final TA:_____

# of Bottles:_____

% Alcohol By Volume:_____

Notes:_____

_____

_____

_____

_____

_____

_____

_____

_____

ATTACH
LABEL
HERE

# TASTING

Color:_____

Body / Flavor:_____

Finish:_____

Tasting Notes:_____

_____

_____

_____

_____

_____

_____

_____

_____

# NOTES FOR NEXT TIME: _____

_____

_____

_____

_____

_____

_____

_____

# PRIMARY FERMENTATION

Date: _____ / _____ / _____     #_____

Name:_____

Ingredients:_____

_____

_____

_____

_____

_____

_____

_____

Yeast:_____

Gallons of Must:_____

Spc.Grv. Before Correction:_____

Sugar Added:_____

Spc.Grv. After Correction:_____

pH Before Correction:_____

pH After Correction:_____

TA Before:_____

TA Correction:_____

TA After:_____

Totas SO2:_____

Notes:_____

_____

_____

_____

_____

# SECONDARY FERMENTATION

| Date | Racked | Spc.Grv. | pH | SO2 | Gallons | Additions |
|------|--------|----------|-----|-----|---------|-----------|
| __ / __ / __ | ☐ | _____ | _____ | _____ | _____ | _____ |
| Notes:_____ | | | | | | |
| __ / __ / __ | ☐ | _____ | _____ | _____ | _____ | _____ |
| Notes:_____ | | | | | | |
| __ / __ / __ | ☐ | _____ | _____ | _____ | _____ | _____ |
| Notes:_____ | | | | | | |
| __ / __ / __ | ☐ | _____ | _____ | _____ | _____ | _____ |
| Notes:_____ | | | | | | |
| __ / __ / __ | ☐ | _____ | _____ | _____ | _____ | _____ |
| Notes:_____ | | | | | | |
| __ / __ / __ | ☐ | _____ | _____ | _____ | _____ | _____ |
| Notes:_____ | | | | | | |

# BOTTLING: _____ / _____ / _____

Spc.Grv. Before Sweetening:_____

Sugar Added:_____

Final pH:_____

Final SO2:_____

Final TA:_____

# of Bottles:_____

% Alcohol By Volume:_____

Notes:_____

_____

_____

_____

_____

_____

_____

_____

_____

_____

> ATTACH
> LABEL
> HERE

# TASTING

Color:_____

Body / Flavor:_____

Finish:_____

Tasting Notes:_____

_____

_____

_____

_____

_____

_____

_____

_____

# NOTES FOR NEXT TIME: _____

_____

_____

_____

_____

_____

_____

# PRIMARY FERMENTATION

Date: _____ / _____ / _____        #_____

Name:_____

Ingredients:_____

_____

_____

_____

_____

_____

_____

_____

Spc.Grv. Before Correction:_____

Sugar Added:_____

Spc.Grv. After Correction:_____

pH Before Correction:_____

pH After Correction:_____

TA Before:_____

TA Correction:_____

Yeast:_____

TA After:_____

Gallons of Must:_____

Totas SO2:_____

Notes:_____

_____

_____

_____

_____

# SECONDARY FERMENTATION

| Date | Racked | Spc.Grv. | pH | SO2 | Gallons | Additions |
|------|--------|----------|-----|-----|---------|-----------|
| __ / __ / __ | ☐ | _____ | _____ | _____ | _____ | _____ |

Notes:_____

_____

| __ / __ / __ | ☐ | _____ | _____ | _____ | _____ | _____ |

Notes:_____

_____

| __ / __ / __ | ☐ | _____ | _____ | _____ | _____ | _____ |

Notes:_____

_____

| __ / __ / __ | ☐ | _____ | _____ | _____ | _____ | _____ |

Notes:_____

_____

| __ / __ / __ | ☐ | _____ | _____ | _____ | _____ | _____ |

Notes:_____

_____

| __ / __ / __ | ☐ | _____ | _____ | _____ | _____ | _____ |

Notes:_____

_____

# BOTTLING: _____ / _____ / _____

Spc.Grv. Before Sweetening:_____

Sugar Added:_____

Final pH:_____

Final SO2:_____

Final TA:_____

# of Bottles:_____

% Alcohol By Volume:_____

Notes:_____

_____

_____

_____

_____

_____

_____

_____

_____

ATTACH
LABEL
HERE

# TASTING

Color:_____

Body / Flavor:_____

Finish:_____

Tasting Notes:_____

_____

_____

_____

_____

_____

_____

_____

# NOTES FOR NEXT TIME: _____

_____

_____

_____

_____

_____

_____

_____

# PRIMARY FERMENTATION

Date: _____ / _____ / _____          #_____

Ingredients:_____

_____

_____

_____

_____

_____

_____

Yeast:_____

Gallons of Must:_____

Notes:_____

_____

_____

_____

Name:_____

Spc.Grv. Before Correction:_____

Sugar Added:_____

Spc.Grv. After Correction:_____

pH Before Correction:_____

pH After Correction:_____

TA Before:_____

TA Correction:_____

TA After:_____

Totas SO2:_____

# SECONDARY FERMENTATION

| Date | Racked | Spc.Grv. | pH | SO2 | Gallons | Additions |
|------|--------|----------|-----|-----|---------|-----------|
| ___ / ___ / ___ | ☐ | _____ | _____ | _____ | _____ | _____ |

Notes:_____

_____

| ___ / ___ / ___ | ☐ | _____ | _____ | _____ | _____ | _____ |

Notes:_____

_____

| ___ / ___ / ___ | ☐ | _____ | _____ | _____ | _____ | _____ |

Notes:_____

_____

| ___ / ___ / ___ | ☐ | _____ | _____ | _____ | _____ | _____ |

Notes:_____

_____

| ___ / ___ / ___ | ☐ | _____ | _____ | _____ | _____ | _____ |

Notes:_____

_____

| ___ / ___ / ___ | ☐ | _____ | _____ | _____ | _____ | _____ |

Notes:_____

_____

# BOTTLING: _____ / _____ / _____

Spc.Grv. Before Sweetening:_____

Sugar Added:_____

Final pH:_____

Final SO2:_____

Final TA:_____

# of Bottles:_____

% Alcohol By Volume:_____

Notes:_____

_____

_____

_____

_____

_____

_____

_____

_____

ATTACH
LABEL
HERE

# TASTING

Color:_____

Body / Flavor:_____

Finish:_____

Tasting Notes:_____

_____

_____

_____

_____

_____

_____

_____

# NOTES FOR NEXT TIME: _____

_____

_____

_____

_____

_____

_____

_____

# PRIMARY FERMENTATION

Date: _____ / _____ / _____     #_____

Ingredients:_____

_____

_____

_____

_____

_____

_____

Yeast:_____

Gallons of Must:_____

Notes:_____

_____

_____

_____

_____

Name:_____

Spc.Grv. Before Correction:_____

Sugar Added:_____

Spc.Grv. After Correction:_____

pH Before Correction:_____

pH After Correction:_____

TA Before:_____

TA Correction:_____

TA After:_____

Totas SO2:_____

# SECONDARY FERMENTATION

| Date | Racked | Spc.Grv. | pH | SO2 | Gallons | Additions |
|------|--------|----------|-----|-----|---------|-----------|
| __ / __ / __ | ☐ | _____ | _____ | _____ | _____ | _____ |

Notes:_____

_____

| __ / __ / __ | ☐ | _____ | _____ | _____ | _____ | _____ |

Notes:_____

_____

| __ / __ / __ | ☐ | _____ | _____ | _____ | _____ | _____ |

Notes:_____

_____

| __ / __ / __ | ☐ | _____ | _____ | _____ | _____ | _____ |

Notes:_____

_____

| __ / __ / __ | ☐ | _____ | _____ | _____ | _____ | _____ |

Notes:_____

_____

| __ / __ / __ | ☐ | _____ | _____ | _____ | _____ | _____ |

Notes:_____

_____

# BOTTLING: _____ / _____ / _____

Spc.Grv. Before Sweetening:_____

Sugar Added:_____

Final pH:_____

Final SO2:_____

Final TA:_____

# of Bottles:_____

% Alcohol By Volume:_____

Notes:_____

_____

_____

_____

_____

_____

_____

_____

ATTACH
LABEL
HERE

# TASTING

Color:_____

Body / Flavor:_____

Finish:_____

Tasting Notes:_____

_____

_____

_____

_____

_____

_____

# NOTES FOR NEXT TIME: _____

_____

_____

_____

_____

_____

_____

# PRIMARY FERMENTATION

Date: _____ / _____ / _____        #_____          Name:_____

Ingredients:_____          Spc.Grv. Before Correction:_____

_____          Sugar Added:_____

_____          Spc.Grv. After Correction:_____

_____          pH Before Correction:_____

_____          pH After Correction:_____

_____          TA Before:_____

_____          TA Correction:_____

Yeast:_____          TA After:_____

Gallons of Must:_____          Totas SO2:_____

Notes:_____

_____

_____

_____

_____

# SECONDARY FERMENTATION

| Date | Racked | Spc.Grv. | pH | SO2 | Gallons | Additions |
|------|--------|----------|-----|-----|---------|-----------|
| __ / __ / __ | ☐ | _____ | _____ | _____ | _____ | _____ |

Notes:_____

_____

| __ / __ / __ | ☐ | _____ | _____ | _____ | _____ | _____ |

Notes:_____

_____

| __ / __ / __ | ☐ | _____ | _____ | _____ | _____ | _____ |

Notes:_____

_____

| __ / __ / __ | ☐ | _____ | _____ | _____ | _____ | _____ |

Notes:_____

_____

| __ / __ / __ | ☐ | _____ | _____ | _____ | _____ | _____ |

Notes:_____

_____

| __ / __ / __ | ☐ | _____ | _____ | _____ | _____ | _____ |

Notes:_____

_____

# BOTTLING: _____ / _____ / _____

Spc.Grv. Before Sweetening:_____

Sugar Added:_____

Final pH:_____

Final SO2:_____

Final TA:_____

# of Bottles:_____

% Alcohol By Volume:_____

Notes:_____

_____

_____

_____

_____

_____

_____

_____

_____

ATTACH
LABEL
HERE

# TASTING

Color:_____

Body / Flavor:_____

Finish:_____

Tasting Notes:_____

_____

_____

_____

_____

_____

_____

_____

# NOTES FOR NEXT TIME: _____

_____

_____

_____

_____

_____

_____

_____

# PRIMARY FERMENTATION

Date: _____ / _____ / _____     #_____     Name:_____

Ingredients:_____     Spc.Grv. Before Correction:_____

_____     Sugar Added:_____

_____     Spc.Grv. After Correction:_____

_____     pH Before Correction:_____

_____     pH After Correction:_____

_____     TA Before:_____

_____     TA Correction:_____

Yeast:_____     TA After:_____

Gallons of Must:_____     Totas SO2:_____

Notes:_____

_____

_____

_____

# SECONDARY FERMENTATION

| Date | Racked | Spc.Grv. | pH | SO2 | Gallons | Additions |
|------|--------|----------|-----|-----|---------|-----------|
| ___ / ___ / ___ | ☐ | _____ | _____ | _____ | _____ | _____ |

Notes:_____

_____

| ___ / ___ / ___ | ☐ | _____ | _____ | _____ | _____ | _____ |

Notes:_____

_____

| ___ / ___ / ___ | ☐ | _____ | _____ | _____ | _____ | _____ |

Notes:_____

_____

| ___ / ___ / ___ | ☐ | _____ | _____ | _____ | _____ | _____ |

Notes:_____

_____

| ___ / ___ / ___ | ☐ | _____ | _____ | _____ | _____ | _____ |

Notes:_____

_____

| ___ / ___ / ___ | ☐ | _____ | _____ | _____ | _____ | _____ |

Notes:_____

_____

# BOTTLING: _____ / _____ / _____

Spc.Grv. Before Sweetening:_____

Sugar Added:_____

Final pH:_____

Final SO2:_____

Final TA:_____

# of Bottles:_____

% Alcohol By Volume:_____

Notes:_____

_____

_____

_____

_____

_____

_____

_____

_____

_____

ATTACH
LABEL
HERE

# TASTING

Color:_____

Body / Flavor:_____

Finish:_____

Tasting Notes:_____

_____

_____

_____

_____

_____

_____

_____

_____

# NOTES FOR NEXT TIME: _____

_____

_____

_____

_____

_____

_____

# PRIMARY FERMENTATION

Date: _____ / _____ / _____          #_____

Name:_____

Ingredients:_____

Spc.Grv. Before Correction:_____

_____

Sugar Added:_____

_____

Spc.Grv. After Correction:_____

_____

pH Before Correction:_____

_____

pH After Correction:_____

_____

TA Before:_____

_____

TA Correction:_____

Yeast:_____

TA After:_____

Gallons of Must:_____

Totas SO2:_____

Notes:_____

_____

_____

_____

# SECONDARY FERMENTATION

| Date | Racked | Spc.Grv. | pH | SO2 | Gallons | Additions |
|------|--------|----------|-----|-----|---------|-----------|
| __ / __ / __ | ☐ | _____ | _____ | _____ | _____ | _____ |

Notes:_____

_____

| __ / __ / __ | ☐ | _____ | _____ | _____ | _____ | _____ |

Notes:_____

_____

| __ / __ / __ | ☐ | _____ | _____ | _____ | _____ | _____ |

Notes:_____

_____

| __ / __ / __ | ☐ | _____ | _____ | _____ | _____ | _____ |

Notes:_____

_____

| __ / __ / __ | ☐ | _____ | _____ | _____ | _____ | _____ |

Notes:_____

_____

| __ / __ / __ | ☐ | _____ | _____ | _____ | _____ | _____ |

Notes:_____

_____

# BOTTLING: _____ / _____ / _____

Spc.Grv. Before Sweetening:_____

Sugar Added:_____

Final pH:_____

Final SO2:_____

Final TA:_____

# of Bottles:_____

% Alcohol By Volume:_____

Notes:_____

_____

_____

_____

_____

_____

_____

_____

_____

Attach Label Here

# TASTING

Color:_____

Body / Flavor:_____

Finish:_____

Tasting Notes:_____

_____

_____

_____

_____

_____

_____

_____

# NOTES FOR NEXT TIME: _____

_____

_____

_____

_____

_____

_____

# PRIMARY FERMENTATION

Date: _____ / _____ / _____          #_____          Name:_____

Ingredients:_____          Spc.Grv. Before Correction:_____

_____          Sugar Added:_____

_____          Spc.Grv. After Correction:_____

_____          pH Before Correction:_____

_____          pH After Correction:_____

_____          TA Before:_____

_____          TA Correction:_____

Yeast:_____          TA After:_____

Gallons of Must:_____          Totas SO2:_____

Notes:_____

_____

_____

_____

# SECONDARY FERMENTATION

| Date | Racked | Spc.Grv. | pH | SO2 | Gallons | Additions |
|------|--------|----------|-----|-----|---------|-----------|
| __ / __ / __ | ☐ | _____ | _____ | _____ | _____ | _____ |

Notes:_____

_____

| __ / __ / __ | ☐ | _____ | _____ | _____ | _____ | _____ |

Notes:_____

_____

| __ / __ / __ | ☐ | _____ | _____ | _____ | _____ | _____ |

Notes:_____

_____

| __ / __ / __ | ☐ | _____ | _____ | _____ | _____ | _____ |

Notes:_____

_____

| __ / __ / __ | ☐ | _____ | _____ | _____ | _____ | _____ |

Notes:_____

_____

| __ / __ / __ | ☐ | _____ | _____ | _____ | _____ | _____ |

Notes:_____

_____

# BOTTLING: _____ /_____ /_____

Spc.Grv. Before Sweetening:_____

Sugar Added:_____

Final pH:_____

Final SO2:_____

Final TA:_____

# of Bottles:_____

% Alcohol By Volume:_____

Notes:_____

_____

_____

_____

_____

_____

_____

_____

_____

ATTACH
LABEL
HERE

# TASTING

Color:_____

Body / Flavor:_____

Finish:_____

Tasting Notes:_____

_____

_____

_____

_____

_____

_____

_____

# NOTES FOR NEXT TIME: _____

_____

_____

_____

_____

_____

_____

# PRIMARY FERMENTATION

Date: _____ / _____ / _____          #_____

Ingredients:_____

_____

_____

_____

_____

_____

_____

Yeast:_____

Gallons of Must:_____

Notes:_____

_____

_____

_____

Name:_____

Spc.Grv. Before Correction:_____

Sugar Added:_____

Spc.Grv. After Correction:_____

pH Before Correction:_____

pH After Correction:_____

TA Before:_____

TA Correction:_____

TA After:_____

Totas SO2:_____

# SECONDARY FERMENTATION

| Date | Racked | Spc.Grv. | pH | SO2 | Gallons | Additions |
|------|--------|----------|-----|-----|---------|-----------|
| ___/___/___ | ☐ | _____ | _____ | _____ | _____ | _____ |

Notes:_____

_____

| ___/___/___ | ☐ | _____ | _____ | _____ | _____ | _____ |

Notes:_____

_____

| ___/___/___ | ☐ | _____ | _____ | _____ | _____ | _____ |

Notes:_____

_____

| ___/___/___ | ☐ | _____ | _____ | _____ | _____ | _____ |

Notes:_____

_____

| ___/___/___ | ☐ | _____ | _____ | _____ | _____ | _____ |

Notes:_____

_____

| ___/___/___ | ☐ | _____ | _____ | _____ | _____ | _____ |

Notes:_____

_____

# BOTTLING: _____ / _____ / _____

Spc.Grv. Before Sweetening:_____

Sugar Added:_____

Final pH:_____

Final SO2:_____

Final TA:_____

# of Bottles:_____

% Alcohol By Volume:_____

Notes:_____

_____

_____

_____

_____

_____

_____

_____

_____

ATTACH LABEL HERE

# TASTING

Color:_____

Body / Flavor:_____

Finish:_____

Tasting Notes:_____

_____

_____

_____

_____

_____

_____

_____

_____

# NOTES FOR NEXT TIME: _____

_____

_____

_____

_____

_____

_____

_____

# PRIMARY FERMENTATION

Date: _____ / _____ / _____          #_____

Name:_____

Ingredients:_____

_____

_____

_____

_____

_____

_____

Yeast:_____

Gallons of Must:_____

Spc.Grv. Before Correction:_____

Sugar Added:_____

Spc.Grv. After Correction:_____

pH Before Correction:_____

pH After Correction:_____

TA Before:_____

TA Correction:_____

TA After:_____

Totas SO2:_____

Notes:_____

_____

_____

_____

_____

# SECONDARY FERMENTATION

| Date | Racked | Spc.Grv. | pH | SO2 | Gallons | Additions |
|------|--------|----------|-----|-----|---------|-----------|
| ___ / ___ / ___ | ☐ | _____ | _____ | _____ | _____ | _____ |

Notes:_____

_____

| ___ / ___ / ___ | ☐ | _____ | _____ | _____ | _____ | _____ |

Notes:_____

_____

| ___ / ___ / ___ | ☐ | _____ | _____ | _____ | _____ | _____ |

Notes:_____

_____

| ___ / ___ / ___ | ☐ | _____ | _____ | _____ | _____ | _____ |

Notes:_____

_____

| ___ / ___ / ___ | ☐ | _____ | _____ | _____ | _____ | _____ |

Notes:_____

_____

| ___ / ___ / ___ | ☐ | _____ | _____ | _____ | _____ | _____ |

Notes:_____

_____

# BOTTLING: _____ / _____ / _____

Spc.Grv. Before Sweetening:_____

Sugar Added:_____

Final pH:_____

Final SO2:_____

Final TA:_____

# of Bottles:_____

% Alcohol By Volume:_____

Notes:_____

_____

_____

_____

_____

_____

_____

_____

_____

ATTACH
LABEL
HERE

# TASTING

Color:_____

Body / Flavor:_____

Finish:_____

Tasting Notes:_____

_____

_____

_____

_____

_____

_____

_____

# NOTES FOR NEXT TIME: _____

_____

_____

_____

_____

_____

_____

_____

# PRIMARY FERMENTATION

Date: _____ / _____ / _____      # _____     Name: _____

Ingredients: _____     Spc.Grv. Before Correction: _____

_____     Sugar Added: _____

_____     Spc.Grv. After Correction: _____

_____     pH Before Correction: _____

_____     pH After Correction: _____

_____     TA Before: _____

_____     TA Correction: _____

Yeast: _____     TA After: _____

Gallons of Must: _____     Totas SO2: _____

Notes: _____

_____

_____

_____

_____

# SECONDARY FERMENTATION

| Date | Racked | Spc.Grv. | pH | SO2 | Gallons | Additions |
|------|--------|----------|-----|-----|---------|-----------|
| __ / __ / __ | ☐ | _____ | _____ | _____ | _____ | _____ |

Notes: _____

_____

| __ / __ / __ | ☐ | _____ | _____ | _____ | _____ | _____ |

Notes: _____

_____

| __ / __ / __ | ☐ | _____ | _____ | _____ | _____ | _____ |

Notes: _____

_____

| __ / __ / __ | ☐ | _____ | _____ | _____ | _____ | _____ |

Notes: _____

_____

| __ / __ / __ | ☐ | _____ | _____ | _____ | _____ | _____ |

Notes: _____

_____

| __ / __ / __ | ☐ | _____ | _____ | _____ | _____ | _____ |

Notes: _____

_____

# BOTTLING: _____ / _____ / _____

Spc.Grv. Before Sweetening:_____

Sugar Added:_____

Final pH:_____

Final SO2:_____

Final TA:_____

# of Bottles:_____

% Alcohol By Volume:_____

Notes:_____

_____

_____

_____

_____

_____

_____

_____

_____

# TASTING

Color:_____

Body / Flavor:_____

Finish:_____

Tasting Notes:_____

_____

_____

_____

_____

_____

_____

_____

# NOTES FOR NEXT TIME: _____

_____

_____

_____

_____

_____

_____

# PRIMARY FERMENTATION

Date: _____ / _____ / _____          #_____

Ingredients:_____

_____

_____

_____

_____

_____

_____

Yeast:_____

Gallons of Must:_____

Notes:_____

_____

_____

_____

_____

Name:_____

Spc.Grv. Before Correction:_____

Sugar Added:_____

Spc.Grv. After Correction:_____

pH Before Correction:_____

pH After Correction:_____

TA Before:_____

TA Correction:_____

TA After:_____

Totas SO2:_____

# SECONDARY FERMENTATION

| Date | Racked | Spc.Grv. | pH | SO2 | Gallons | Additions |
|------|--------|----------|-----|-----|---------|-----------|
| __ / __ / __ | ☐ | _____ | _____ | _____ | _____ | _____ |

Notes:_____

_____

| __ / __ / __ | ☐ | _____ | _____ | _____ | _____ | _____ |

Notes:_____

_____

| __ / __ / __ | ☐ | _____ | _____ | _____ | _____ | _____ |

Notes:_____

_____

| __ / __ / __ | ☐ | _____ | _____ | _____ | _____ | _____ |

Notes:_____

_____

| __ / __ / __ | ☐ | _____ | _____ | _____ | _____ | _____ |

Notes:_____

_____

| __ / __ / __ | ☐ | _____ | _____ | _____ | _____ | _____ |

Notes:_____

_____

# BOTTLING: _____ / _____ / _____

Spc.Grv. Before Sweetening:_____

Sugar Added:_____

Final pH:_____

Final SO2:_____

Final TA:_____

# of Bottles:_____

% Alcohol By Volume:_____

Notes:_____

_____

_____

_____

_____

_____

_____

_____

ATTACH
LABEL
HERE

_____

_____

# TASTING

Color:_____

Body / Flavor:_____

Finish:_____

Tasting Notes:_____

_____

_____

_____

_____

_____

_____

_____

# NOTES FOR NEXT TIME: _____

_____

_____

_____

_____

_____

_____

# PRIMARY FERMENTATION

Date: _____ / _____ / _____          #_____

Ingredients:_____

_____

_____

_____

_____

_____

_____

_____

Yeast:_____

Gallons of Must:_____

Notes:_____

_____

_____

_____

_____

Name:_____

Spc.Grv. Before Correction:_____

Sugar Added:_____

Spc.Grv. After Correction:_____

pH Before Correction:_____

pH After Correction:_____

TA Before:_____

TA Correction:_____

TA After:_____

Totas SO2:_____

# SECONDARY FERMENTATION

| Date | Racked | Spc.Grv. | pH | SO2 | Gallons | Additions |
|------|--------|----------|-----|-----|---------|-----------|
| ___ / ___ / ___ | ☐ | _____ | _____ | _____ | _____ | _____ |

Notes:_____

_____

| ___ / ___ / ___ | ☐ | _____ | _____ | _____ | _____ | _____ |

Notes:_____

_____

| ___ / ___ / ___ | ☐ | _____ | _____ | _____ | _____ | _____ |

Notes:_____

_____

| ___ / ___ / ___ | ☐ | _____ | _____ | _____ | _____ | _____ |

Notes:_____

_____

| ___ / ___ / ___ | ☐ | _____ | _____ | _____ | _____ | _____ |

Notes:_____

_____

| ___ / ___ / ___ | ☐ | _____ | _____ | _____ | _____ | _____ |

Notes:_____

_____

# BOTTLING: _____ / _____ / _____

Spc.Grv. Before Sweetening:_____

Sugar Added:_____

Final pH:_____

Final SO2:_____

Final TA:_____

# of Bottles:_____

% Alcohol By Volume:_____

Notes:_____

_____

_____

_____

_____

_____

_____

_____

ATTACH
LABEL
HERE

_____

_____

# TASTING

Color:_____

Body / Flavor:_____

Finish:_____

Tasting Notes:_____

_____

_____

_____

_____

_____

_____

_____

_____

# NOTES FOR NEXT TIME: _____

_____

_____

_____

_____

_____

_____

_____

# PRIMARY FERMENTATION

Date: _____ / _____ / _____     #_____

Name:_____

Ingredients:_____

Spc.Grv. Before Correction:_____

_____

Sugar Added:_____

_____

Spc.Grv. After Correction:_____

_____

pH Before Correction:_____

_____

pH After Correction:_____

_____

TA Before:_____

_____

TA Correction:_____

_____

Yeast:_____

TA After:_____

Gallons of Must:_____

Totas SO2:_____

Notes:_____

_____

_____

_____

_____

# SECONDARY FERMENTATION

| Date | Racked | Spc.Grv. | pH | SO2 | Gallons | Additions |
|------|--------|----------|-----|-----|---------|-----------|
| __/__/__ | ☐ | _____ | _____ | _____ | _____ | _____ |

Notes:_____

_____

| __/__/__ | ☐ | _____ | _____ | _____ | _____ | _____ |

Notes:_____

_____

| __/__/__ | ☐ | _____ | _____ | _____ | _____ | _____ |

Notes:_____

_____

| __/__/__ | ☐ | _____ | _____ | _____ | _____ | _____ |

Notes:_____

_____

| __/__/__ | ☐ | _____ | _____ | _____ | _____ | _____ |

Notes:_____

_____

| __/__/__ | ☐ | _____ | _____ | _____ | _____ | _____ |

Notes:_____

_____

# BOTTLING: _____ / _____ / _____

Spc.Grv. Before Sweetening:_____

Sugar Added:_____

Final pH:_____

Final SO2:_____

Final TA:_____

# of Bottles:_____

% Alcohol By Volume:_____

Notes:_____

_____

_____

_____

_____

_____

_____

_____

_____

ATTACH LABEL HERE

# TASTING

Color:_____

Body / Flavor:_____

Finish:_____

Tasting Notes:_____

_____

_____

_____

_____

_____

_____

_____

# NOTES FOR NEXT TIME: _____

_____

_____

_____

_____

_____

_____

# PRIMARY FERMENTATION

Date: _____ / _____ / _____     # _____     Name: _____

Ingredients: _____     Spc.Grv. Before Correction: _____

_____     Sugar Added: _____

_____     Spc.Grv. After Correction: _____

_____     pH Before Correction: _____

_____     pH After Correction: _____

_____     TA Before: _____

_____     TA Correction: _____

Yeast: _____     TA After: _____

Gallons of Must: _____     Totas SO2: _____

Notes: _____

_____

_____

_____

_____

# SECONDARY FERMENTATION

| Date | Racked | Spc.Grv. | pH | SO2 | Gallons | Additions |
|------|--------|----------|-----|-----|---------|-----------|
| __ / __ / __ | ☐ | _____ | _____ | _____ | _____ | _____ |

Notes: _____

_____

| __ / __ / __ | ☐ | _____ | _____ | _____ | _____ | _____ |

Notes: _____

_____

| __ / __ / __ | ☐ | _____ | _____ | _____ | _____ | _____ |

Notes: _____

_____

| __ / __ / __ | ☐ | _____ | _____ | _____ | _____ | _____ |

Notes: _____

_____

| __ / __ / __ | ☐ | _____ | _____ | _____ | _____ | _____ |

Notes: _____

_____

| __ / __ / __ | ☐ | _____ | _____ | _____ | _____ | _____ |

Notes: _____

_____

# BOTTLING: _____ / _____ / _____

Spc.Grv. Before Sweetening:_____

Sugar Added:_____

Final pH:_____

Final SO2:_____

Final TA:_____

# of Bottles:_____

% Alcohol By Volume:_____

Notes:_____

_____

_____

_____

_____

_____

_____

_____

_____

Attach Label Here

# TASTING

Color:_____

Body / Flavor:_____

Finish:_____

Tasting Notes:_____

_____

_____

_____

_____

_____

_____

_____

# NOTES FOR NEXT TIME: _____

_____

_____

_____

_____

_____

_____

# PRIMARY FERMENTATION

Date: _____ / _____ / _____     #_____     Name:_____

Ingredients:_____     Spc.Grv. Before Correction:_____

_____     Sugar Added:_____

_____     Spc.Grv. After Correction:_____

_____     pH Before Correction:_____

_____     pH After Correction:_____

_____     TA Before:_____

_____     TA Correction:_____

_____     TA After:_____

Yeast:_____     TotasSO2:_____

Gallons of Must:_____

Notes:_____

_____

_____

_____

# SECONDARY FERMENTATION

| Date | Racked | Spc.Grv. | pH | SO2 | Gallons | Additions |
|------|--------|----------|-----|-----|---------|-----------|
| __ / __ / __ | ☐ | _____ | _____ | _____ | _____ | _____ |

Notes:_____

_____

| __ / __ / __ | ☐ | _____ | _____ | _____ | _____ | _____ |

Notes:_____

_____

| __ / __ / __ | ☐ | _____ | _____ | _____ | _____ | _____ |

Notes:_____

_____

| __ / __ / __ | ☐ | _____ | _____ | _____ | _____ | _____ |

Notes:_____

_____

| __ / __ / __ | ☐ | _____ | _____ | _____ | _____ | _____ |

Notes:_____

_____

| __ / __ / __ | ☐ | _____ | _____ | _____ | _____ | _____ |

Notes:_____

_____

# BOTTLING: _____ / _____ / _____

Spc.Grv. Before Sweetening:_____

Sugar Added:_____

Final pH:_____

Final SO2:_____

Final TA:_____

# of Bottles:_____

% Alcohol By Volume:_____


Notes:_____

_____

_____

_____

_____

_____

_____

_____

_____

ATTACH
LABEL
HERE

# TASTING

Color:_____

Body / Flavor:_____

Finish:_____

Tasting Notes:_____

_____

_____

_____

_____

_____

_____

_____

# NOTES FOR NEXT TIME: _____

_____

_____

_____

_____

_____

_____

_____

# PRIMARY FERMENTATION

Date: _____ / _____ / _____     #_____

Ingredients:_____

_____

_____

_____

_____

_____

_____

Yeast:_____

Gallons of Must:_____

Notes:_____

_____

_____

_____

_____

Name:_____

Spc.Grv. Before Correction:_____

Sugar Added:_____

Spc.Grv. After Correction:_____

pH Before Correction:_____

pH After Correction:_____

TA Before:_____

TA Correction:_____

TA After:_____

Totas SO2:_____

# SECONDARY FERMENTATION

| Date | Racked | Spc.Grv. | pH | SO2 | Gallons | Additions |
|------|--------|----------|-----|-----|---------|-----------|
| __ / __ / __ | ☐ | _____ | _____ | _____ | _____ | _____ |

Notes:_____

_____

| __ / __ / __ | ☐ | _____ | _____ | _____ | _____ | _____ |

Notes:_____

_____

| __ / __ / __ | ☐ | _____ | _____ | _____ | _____ | _____ |

Notes:_____

_____

| __ / __ / __ | ☐ | _____ | _____ | _____ | _____ | _____ |

Notes:_____

_____

| __ / __ / __ | ☐ | _____ | _____ | _____ | _____ | _____ |

Notes:_____

_____

| __ / __ / __ | ☐ | _____ | _____ | _____ | _____ | _____ |

Notes:_____

_____

# BOTTLING: _____ / _____ / _____

Spc.Grv. Before Sweetening:_____

Sugar Added:_____

Final pH:_____

Final SO2:_____

Final TA:_____

# of Bottles:_____

% Alcohol By Volume:_____

Notes:_____
_____
_____
_____
_____
_____
_____
_____
_____

ATTACH
LABEL
HERE

# TASTING

Color:_____

Body / Flavor:_____

Finish:_____

Tasting Notes:_____
_____
_____
_____
_____
_____
_____
_____

# NOTES FOR NEXT TIME: _____
_____
_____
_____
_____
_____
_____

# PRIMARY FERMENTATION

Date: _____ / _____ / _____        #_____

Ingredients:_____

_____

_____

_____

_____

_____

_____

_____

Yeast:_____

Gallons of Must:_____

Notes:_____

_____

_____

_____

_____

Name:_____

Spc.Grv. Before Correction:_____

Sugar Added:_____

Spc.Grv. After Correction:_____

pH Before Correction:_____

pH After Correction:_____

TA Before:_____

TA Correction:_____

TA After:_____

Totas SO2:_____

# SECONDARY FERMENTATION

| Date | Racked | Spc.Grv. | pH | SO2 | Gallons | Additions |
|------|--------|----------|-----|-----|---------|-----------|
| __ / __ / __ | ☐ | _____ | _____ | _____ | _____ | _____ |

Notes:_____

_____

| __ / __ / __ | ☐ | _____ | _____ | _____ | _____ | _____ |

Notes:_____

_____

| __ / __ / __ | ☐ | _____ | _____ | _____ | _____ | _____ |

Notes:_____

_____

| __ / __ / __ | ☐ | _____ | _____ | _____ | _____ | _____ |

Notes:_____

_____

| __ / __ / __ | ☐ | _____ | _____ | _____ | _____ | _____ |

Notes:_____

_____

| __ / __ / __ | ☐ | _____ | _____ | _____ | _____ | _____ |

Notes:_____

_____

# BOTTLING: _____ / _____ / _____

Spc.Grv. Before Sweetening:_____

Sugar Added:_____

Final pH:_____

Final SO2:_____

Final TA:_____

# of Bottles:_____

% Alcohol By Volume:_____

Notes:_____

_____

_____

_____

_____

_____

_____

_____

_____

_____

ATTACH
LABEL
HERE

# TASTING

Color:_____

Body / Flavor:_____

Finish:_____

Tasting Notes:_____

_____

_____

_____

_____

_____

_____

_____

# NOTES FOR NEXT TIME: _____

_____

_____

_____

_____

_____

_____

_____

# PRIMARY FERMENTATION

Date: _____ / _____ / _____     #_____

Name:_____

Ingredients:_____

Spc.Grv. Before Correction:_____

_____

Sugar Added:_____

_____

Spc.Grv. After Correction:_____

_____

pH Before Correction:_____

_____

pH After Correction:_____

_____

TA Before:_____

_____

TA Correction:_____

_____

Yeast:_____

TA After:_____

Gallons of Must:_____

Totas SO2:_____

Notes:_____

_____

_____

_____

_____

# SECONDARY FERMENTATION

| Date | Racked | Spc.Grv. | pH | SO2 | Gallons | Additions |
|------|--------|----------|-----|-----|---------|-----------|
| __/__/__ | ☐ | _____ | _____ | _____ | _____ | _____ |
| Notes: | | | | | | |
| __/__/__ | ☐ | _____ | _____ | _____ | _____ | _____ |
| Notes: | | | | | | |
| __/__/__ | ☐ | _____ | _____ | _____ | _____ | _____ |
| Notes: | | | | | | |
| __/__/__ | ☐ | _____ | _____ | _____ | _____ | _____ |
| Notes: | | | | | | |
| __/__/__ | ☐ | _____ | _____ | _____ | _____ | _____ |
| Notes: | | | | | | |
| __/__/__ | ☐ | _____ | _____ | _____ | _____ | _____ |
| Notes: | | | | | | |

# BOTTLING: _____ / _____ / _____

Spc.Grv. Before Sweetening:_____

Sugar Added:_____

Final pH:_____

Final SO2:_____

Final TA:_____

# of Bottles:_____

% Alcohol By Volume:_____

Notes:_____
_____
_____
_____
_____
_____
_____
_____
_____

Attach Label Here

# TASTING

Color:_____

Body / Flavor:_____

Finish:_____

Tasting Notes:_____
_____
_____
_____
_____
_____
_____
_____

# NOTES FOR NEXT TIME: _____
_____
_____
_____
_____
_____
_____

# PRIMARY FERMENTATION

Date: _____ / _____ / _____          #_____

Name:_____

Ingredients:_____

_____

Spc.Grv. Before Correction:_____

_____

Sugar Added:_____

_____

Spc.Grv. After Correction:_____

_____

pH Before Correction:_____

_____

pH After Correction:_____

_____

TA Before:_____

_____

TA Correction:_____

Yeast:_____

TA After:_____

Gallons of Must:_____

Totas SO2:_____

Notes:_____

_____

_____

_____

_____

# SECONDARY FERMENTATION

| Date | Racked | Spc.Grv. | pH | SO2 | Gallons | Additions |
|------|--------|----------|-----|-----|---------|-----------|
| ___/___/___ | ☐ | _____ | _____ | _____ | _____ | _____ |

Notes:_____

_____

| ___/___/___ | ☐ | _____ | _____ | _____ | _____ | _____ |

Notes:_____

_____

| ___/___/___ | ☐ | _____ | _____ | _____ | _____ | _____ |

Notes:_____

_____

| ___/___/___ | ☐ | _____ | _____ | _____ | _____ | _____ |

Notes:_____

_____

| ___/___/___ | ☐ | _____ | _____ | _____ | _____ | _____ |

Notes:_____

_____

| ___/___/___ | ☐ | _____ | _____ | _____ | _____ | _____ |

Notes:_____

_____

# BOTTLING: _____ / _____ / _____

Spc.Grv. Before Sweetening:_____

Sugar Added:_____

Final pH:_____

Final SO2:_____

Final TA:_____

# of Bottles:_____

% Alcohol By Volume:_____

Notes:_____

_____

_____

_____

_____

_____

_____

_____

_____

_____

ATTACH LABEL HERE

# TASTING

Color:_____

Body / Flavor:_____

Finish:_____

Tasting Notes:_____

_____

_____

_____

_____

_____

_____

_____

_____

# NOTES FOR NEXT TIME: _____

_____

_____

_____

_____

_____

_____

_____

# PRIMARY FERMENTATION

Date: _____ / _____ / _____     #_____

Ingredients:_____

_____

_____

_____

_____

_____

_____

Yeast:_____

Gallons of Must:_____

Notes:_____

_____

_____

_____

_____

Name:_____

Spc.Grv. Before Correction:_____

Sugar Added:_____

Spc.Grv. After Correction:_____

pH Before Correction:_____

pH After Correction:_____

TA Before:_____

TA Correction:_____

TA After:_____

Totas SO2:_____

# SECONDARY FERMENTATION

| Date | Racked | Spc.Grv. | pH | SO2 | Gallons | Additions |
|------|--------|----------|-----|-----|---------|-----------|
| ___ / ___ / ___ | ☐ | _____ | _____ | _____ | _____ | _____ |

Notes:_____

_____

| ___ / ___ / ___ | ☐ | _____ | _____ | _____ | _____ | _____ |

Notes:_____

_____

| ___ / ___ / ___ | ☐ | _____ | _____ | _____ | _____ | _____ |

Notes:_____

_____

| ___ / ___ / ___ | ☐ | _____ | _____ | _____ | _____ | _____ |

Notes:_____

_____

| ___ / ___ / ___ | ☐ | _____ | _____ | _____ | _____ | _____ |

Notes:_____

_____

| ___ / ___ / ___ | ☐ | _____ | _____ | _____ | _____ | _____ |

Notes:_____

_____

# BOTTLING: _____ / _____ / _____

Spc.Grv. Before Sweetening:_____

Sugar Added:_____

Final pH:_____

Final SO2:_____

Final TA:_____

# of Bottles:_____

% Alcohol By Volume:_____


Notes:_____

_____

_____

_____

_____

_____

_____

_____

_____

> ATTACH
> LABEL
> HERE

# TASTING

Color:_____

Body / Flavor:_____

Finish:_____

Tasting Notes:_____

_____

_____

_____

_____

_____

_____

_____

_____

# NOTES FOR NEXT TIME: _____

_____

_____

_____

_____

_____

_____

# PRIMARY FERMENTATION

Date: _____ / _____ / _____          #_____

Ingredients:_____

_____

_____

_____

_____

_____

_____

Yeast:_____

Gallons of Must:_____

Notes:_____

_____

_____

_____

_____

Name:_____

Spc.Grv. Before Correction:_____

Sugar Added:_____

Spc.Grv. After Correction:_____

pH Before Correction:_____

pH After Correction:_____

TA Before:_____

TA Correction:_____

TA After:_____

Totas SO2:_____

# SECONDARY FERMENTATION

| Date | Racked | Spc.Grv. | pH | SO2 | Gallons | Additions |
|------|--------|----------|-----|-----|---------|-----------|
| __ / __ / __ | ☐ | _____ | _____ | _____ | _____ | _____ |

Notes:_____

_____

| __ / __ / __ | ☐ | _____ | _____ | _____ | _____ | _____ |

Notes:_____

_____

| __ / __ / __ | ☐ | _____ | _____ | _____ | _____ | _____ |

Notes:_____

_____

| __ / __ / __ | ☐ | _____ | _____ | _____ | _____ | _____ |

Notes:_____

_____

| __ / __ / __ | ☐ | _____ | _____ | _____ | _____ | _____ |

Notes:_____

_____

| __ / __ / __ | ☐ | _____ | _____ | _____ | _____ | _____ |

Notes:_____

_____

# BOTTLING: _____ / _____ / _____

Spc.Grv. Before Sweetening:_____

Sugar Added:_____

Final pH:_____

Final SO2:_____

Final TA:_____

# of Bottles:_____

% Alcohol By Volume:_____

Notes:_____

_____

_____

_____

_____

_____

_____

ATTACH
LABEL
HERE

_____

_____

# TASTING

Color:_____

Body / Flavor:_____

Finish:_____

Tasting Notes:_____

_____

_____

_____

_____

_____

_____

_____

# NOTES FOR NEXT TIME: _____

_____

_____

_____

_____

_____

_____

# PRIMARY FERMENTATION

Date: _____ / _____ / _____       #_____

Ingredients:_____

_____

_____

_____

_____

_____

_____

Yeast:_____

Gallons of Must:_____

Notes:_____

_____

_____

_____

_____

Name:_____

Spc.Grv. Before Correction:_____

Sugar Added:_____

Spc.Grv. After Correction:_____

pH Before Correction:_____

pH After Correction:_____

TA Before:_____

TA Correction:_____

TA After:_____

Totas SO2:_____

# SECONDARY FERMENTATION

| Date | Racked | Spc.Grv. | pH | SO2 | Gallons | Additions |
|------|--------|----------|-----|-----|---------|-----------|
| ___/___/___ | ☐ | _____ | _____ | _____ | _____ | _____ |

Notes:_____

_____

| ___/___/___ | ☐ | _____ | _____ | _____ | _____ | _____ |

Notes:_____

_____

| ___/___/___ | ☐ | _____ | _____ | _____ | _____ | _____ |

Notes:_____

_____

| ___/___/___ | ☐ | _____ | _____ | _____ | _____ | _____ |

Notes:_____

_____

| ___/___/___ | ☐ | _____ | _____ | _____ | _____ | _____ |

Notes:_____

_____

| ___/___/___ | ☐ | _____ | _____ | _____ | _____ | _____ |

Notes:_____

_____

# BOTTLING: _____ / _____ / _____

Spc.Grv. Before Sweetening:_____

Sugar Added:_____

Final pH:_____

Final SO2:_____

Final TA:_____

# of Bottles:_____

% Alcohol By Volume:_____

Notes:_____

_____

_____

_____

_____

_____

_____

ATTACH
LABEL
HERE

_____

_____

# TASTING

Color:_____

Body / Flavor:_____

Finish:_____

Tasting Notes:_____

_____

_____

_____

_____

_____

_____

_____

# NOTES FOR NEXT TIME: _____

_____

_____

_____

_____

_____

_____

# PRIMARY FERMENTATION

Date: _____ / _____ / _____     #_____

Name:_____

Ingredients:_____

Spc.Grv. Before Correction:_____

_____

Sugar Added:_____

_____

Spc.Grv. After Correction:_____

_____

pH Before Correction:_____

_____

pH After Correction:_____

_____

TA Before:_____

_____

TA Correction:_____

Yeast:_____

TA After:_____

Gallons of Must:_____

Totas SO2:_____

Notes:_____

_____

_____

_____

# SECONDARY FERMENTATION

| Date | Racked | Spc.Grv. | pH | SO2 | Gallons | Additions |
|------|--------|----------|-----|-----|---------|-----------|
| ___/___/___ | ☐ | _____ | _____ | _____ | _____ | _____ |

Notes:_____

_____

| ___/___/___ | ☐ | _____ | _____ | _____ | _____ | _____ |

Notes:_____

_____

| ___/___/___ | ☐ | _____ | _____ | _____ | _____ | _____ |

Notes:_____

_____

| ___/___/___ | ☐ | _____ | _____ | _____ | _____ | _____ |

Notes:_____

_____

| ___/___/___ | ☐ | _____ | _____ | _____ | _____ | _____ |

Notes:_____

_____

| ___/___/___ | ☐ | _____ | _____ | _____ | _____ | _____ |

Notes:_____

_____

# BOTTLING: _____ / _____ / _____

Spc.Grv. Before Sweetening:_____

Sugar Added:_____

Final pH:_____

Final SO2:_____

Final TA:_____

# of Bottles:_____

% Alcohol By Volume:_____

Notes:_____

_____

_____

_____

_____

_____

_____

_____

_____

_____

ATTACH
LABEL
HERE

# TASTING

Color:_____

Body / Flavor:_____

Finish:_____

Tasting Notes:_____

_____

_____

_____

_____

_____

_____

_____

# NOTES FOR NEXT TIME: _____

_____

_____

_____

_____

_____

_____

# PRIMARY FERMENTATION

Date: _____ / _____ / _____      #_____

Ingredients:_____

_____

_____

_____

_____

_____

_____

Yeast:_____

Gallons of Must:_____

Notes:_____

_____

_____

_____

_____

Name:_____

Spc.Grv. Before Correction:_____

Sugar Added:_____

Spc.Grv. After Correction:_____

pH Before Correction:_____

pH After Correction:_____

TA Before:_____

TA Correction:_____

TA After:_____

Totas SO2:_____

# SECONDARY FERMENTATION

| Date | Racked | Spc.Grv. | pH | SO2 | Gallons | Additions |
|------|--------|----------|-----|-----|---------|-----------|
| __ / __ / __ | ☐ | _____ | _____ | _____ | _____ | _____ |

Notes:_____

_____

| __ / __ / __ | ☐ | _____ | _____ | _____ | _____ | _____ |

Notes:_____

_____

| __ / __ / __ | ☐ | _____ | _____ | _____ | _____ | _____ |

Notes:_____

_____

| __ / __ / __ | ☐ | _____ | _____ | _____ | _____ | _____ |

Notes:_____

_____

| __ / __ / __ | ☐ | _____ | _____ | _____ | _____ | _____ |

Notes:_____

_____

| __ / __ / __ | ☐ | _____ | _____ | _____ | _____ | _____ |

Notes:_____

_____

# BOTTLING: _____ / _____ / _____

Spc.Grv. Before Sweetening:_____

Sugar Added:_____

Final pH:_____

Final SO2:_____

Final TA:_____

# of Bottles:_____

% Alcohol By Volume:_____

Notes:_____

_____

_____

_____

_____

_____

_____

_____

_____

Attach
Label
Here

# TASTING

Color:_____

Body / Flavor:_____

Finish:_____

Tasting Notes:_____

_____

_____

_____

_____

_____

_____

_____

# NOTES FOR NEXT TIME: _____

_____

_____

_____

_____

_____

_____

# PRIMARY FERMENTATION

Date: _____ / _____ / _____          #_____

Name:_____

Ingredients:_____

Spc.Grv. Before Correction:_____

_____

Sugar Added:_____

_____

Spc.Grv. After Correction:_____

_____

pH Before Correction:_____

_____

pH After Correction:_____

_____

TA Before:_____

_____

TA Correction:_____

Yeast:_____

TA After:_____

Gallons of Must:_____

Totas SO2:_____

Notes:_____

_____

_____

_____

# SECONDARY FERMENTATION

| Date | Racked | Spc.Grv. | pH | SO2 | Gallons | Additions |
|------|--------|----------|-----|-----|---------|-----------|
| __ / __ / __ | ☐ | _____ | _____ | _____ | _____ | _____ |

Notes:_____

_____

| __ / __ / __ | ☐ | _____ | _____ | _____ | _____ | _____ |

Notes:_____

_____

| __ / __ / __ | ☐ | _____ | _____ | _____ | _____ | _____ |

Notes:_____

_____

| __ / __ / __ | ☐ | _____ | _____ | _____ | _____ | _____ |

Notes:_____

_____

| __ / __ / __ | ☐ | _____ | _____ | _____ | _____ | _____ |

Notes:_____

_____

| __ / __ / __ | ☐ | _____ | _____ | _____ | _____ | _____ |

Notes:_____

_____

# BOTTLING: _____ /_____ /_____

Spc.Grv. Before Sweetening:_____

Sugar Added:_____

Final pH:_____

Final SO2:_____

Final TA:_____

# of Bottles:_____

% Alcohol By Volume:_____

Notes:_____

_____

_____

_____

_____

_____

_____

_____

_____

ATTACH
LABEL
HERE

# TASTING

Color:_____

Body / Flavor:_____

Finish:_____

Tasting Notes:_____

_____

_____

_____

_____

_____

_____

_____

# NOTES FOR NEXT TIME: _____

_____

_____

_____

_____

_____

_____

# PRIMARY FERMENTATION

Date: _____ / _____ / _____          #_____

Ingredients:_____

_____

_____

_____

_____

_____

Yeast:_____

Gallons of Must:_____

Notes:_____

_____

_____

_____

_____

Name:_____

Spc.Grv. Before Correction:_____

Sugar Added:_____

Spc.Grv. After Correction:_____

pH Before Correction:_____

pH After Correction:_____

TA Before:_____

TA Correction:_____

TA After:_____

Totas SO2:_____

# SECONDARY FERMENTATION

| Date | Racked | Spc.Grv. | pH | SO2 | Gallons | Additions |
|------|--------|----------|-----|-----|---------|-----------|
| ___ / ___ / ___ | ☐ | _____ | _____ | _____ | _____ | _____ |

Notes:_____

_____

| ___ / ___ / ___ | ☐ | _____ | _____ | _____ | _____ | _____ |

Notes:_____

_____

| ___ / ___ / ___ | ☐ | _____ | _____ | _____ | _____ | _____ |

Notes:_____

_____

| ___ / ___ / ___ | ☐ | _____ | _____ | _____ | _____ | _____ |

Notes:_____

_____

| ___ / ___ / ___ | ☐ | _____ | _____ | _____ | _____ | _____ |

Notes:_____

_____

| ___ / ___ / ___ | ☐ | _____ | _____ | _____ | _____ | _____ |

Notes:_____

_____

# BOTTLING: _____ / _____ / _____

Spc.Grv. Before Sweetening:_____

Sugar Added:_____

Final pH:_____

Final SO2:_____

Final TA:_____

# of Bottles:_____

% Alcohol By Volume:_____

Notes:_____

_____

_____

_____

_____

_____

_____

_____

_____

ATTACH
LABEL
HERE

# TASTING

Color:_____

Body / Flavor:_____

Finish:_____

Tasting Notes:_____

_____

_____

_____

_____

_____

_____

_____

# NOTES FOR NEXT TIME: _____

_____

_____

_____

_____

_____

_____

# PRIMARY FERMENTATION

Date: _____ / _____ / _____          #_____

Ingredients:_____

_____

_____

_____

_____

_____

_____

Yeast:_____

Gallons of Must:_____

Name:_____

Spc.Grv. Before Correction:_____

Sugar Added:_____

Spc.Grv. After Correction:_____

pH Before Correction:_____

pH After Correction:_____

TA Before:_____

TA Correction:_____

TA After:_____

Totas SO2:_____

Notes:_____

_____

_____

_____

_____

# SECONDARY FERMENTATION

| Date | Racked | Spc.Grv. | pH | SO2 | Gallons | Additions |
|------|--------|----------|-----|-----|---------|-----------|
| __ / __ / __ | ☐ | _____ | _____ | _____ | _____ | _____ |

Notes:_____

_____

| __ / __ / __ | ☐ | _____ | _____ | _____ | _____ | _____ |

Notes:_____

_____

| __ / __ / __ | ☐ | _____ | _____ | _____ | _____ | _____ |

Notes:_____

_____

| __ / __ / __ | ☐ | _____ | _____ | _____ | _____ | _____ |

Notes:_____

_____

| __ / __ / __ | ☐ | _____ | _____ | _____ | _____ | _____ |

Notes:_____

_____

| __ / __ / __ | ☐ | _____ | _____ | _____ | _____ | _____ |

Notes:_____

_____

# BOTTLING: _____ / _____ / _____

Spc.Grv. Before Sweetening:_____

Sugar Added:_____

Final pH:_____

Final SO2:_____

Final TA:_____

# of Bottles:_____

% Alcohol By Volume:_____


Notes:_____

_____

_____

_____

_____

_____

_____

_____

Attach Label Here

# TASTING

Color:_____

Body / Flavor:_____

Finish:_____

Tasting Notes:_____

_____

_____

_____

_____

_____

_____

_____

_____

# NOTES FOR NEXT TIME: _____

_____

_____

_____

_____

_____

_____

_____

# PRIMARY FERMENTATION

Date: _____ / _____ / _____      #_____

Ingredients:_____

_____

_____

_____

_____

_____

_____

Yeast:_____

Gallons of Must:_____

Notes:_____

_____

_____

_____

_____

Name:_____

Spc.Grv. Before Correction:_____

Sugar Added:_____

Spc.Grv. After Correction:_____

pH Before Correction:_____

pH After Correction:_____

TA Before:_____

TA Correction:_____

TA After:_____

Totas SO2:_____

# SECONDARY FERMENTATION

| Date | Racked | Spc.Grv. | pH | SO2 | Gallons | Additions |
|------|--------|----------|-----|-----|---------|-----------|
| __ / __ / __ | ☐ | _____ | _____ | _____ | _____ | _____ |

Notes:_____

_____

| __ / __ / __ | ☐ | _____ | _____ | _____ | _____ | _____ |

Notes:_____

_____

| __ / __ / __ | ☐ | _____ | _____ | _____ | _____ | _____ |

Notes:_____

_____

| __ / __ / __ | ☐ | _____ | _____ | _____ | _____ | _____ |

Notes:_____

_____

| __ / __ / __ | ☐ | _____ | _____ | _____ | _____ | _____ |

Notes:_____

_____

| __ / __ / __ | ☐ | _____ | _____ | _____ | _____ | _____ |

Notes:_____

_____

# BOTTLING: _____ / _____ / _____

Spc.Grv. Before Sweetening:_____

Sugar Added:_____

Final pH:_____

Final SO2:_____

Final TA:_____

# of Bottles:_____

% Alcohol By Volume:_____

Notes:_____

_____

_____

_____

_____

_____

_____

ATTACH
LABEL
HERE

_____

_____

# TASTING

Color:_____

Body / Flavor:_____

Finish:_____

Tasting Notes:_____

_____

_____

_____

_____

_____

_____

_____

_____

# NOTES FOR NEXT TIME: _____

_____

_____

_____

_____

_____

_____

# PRIMARY FERMENTATION

Date: _____ / _____ / _____          #_____

Ingredients:_____

_____

_____

_____

_____

_____

_____

Yeast:_____

Gallons of Must:_____

Notes:_____

_____

_____

_____

_____

Name:_____

Spc.Grv. Before Correction:_____

Sugar Added:_____

Spc.Grv. After Correction:_____

pH Before Correction:_____

pH After Correction:_____

TA Before:_____

TA Correction:_____

TA After:_____

Totas SO2:_____

# SECONDARY FERMENTATION

| Date | Racked | Spc.Grv. | pH | SO2 | Gallons | Additions |
|------|--------|----------|-----|-----|---------|-----------|
| __ / __ / __ | ☐ | _____ | _____ | _____ | _____ | _____ |

Notes:_____

_____

| __ / __ / __ | ☐ | _____ | _____ | _____ | _____ | _____ |

Notes:_____

_____

| __ / __ / __ | ☐ | _____ | _____ | _____ | _____ | _____ |

Notes:_____

_____

| __ / __ / __ | ☐ | _____ | _____ | _____ | _____ | _____ |

Notes:_____

_____

| __ / __ / __ | ☐ | _____ | _____ | _____ | _____ | _____ |

Notes:_____

_____

| __ / __ / __ | ☐ | _____ | _____ | _____ | _____ | _____ |

Notes:_____

_____

# BOTTLING: _____ / _____ / _____

Spc.Grv. Before Sweetening:_____

Sugar Added:_____

Final pH:_____

Final SO2:_____

Final TA:_____

# of Bottles:_____

% Alcohol By Volume:_____

Notes:_____

_____

_____

_____

_____

_____

_____

_____

_____

ATTACH
LABEL
HERE

# TASTING

Color:_____

Body / Flavor:_____

Finish:_____

Tasting Notes:_____

_____

_____

_____

_____

_____

_____

_____

# NOTES FOR NEXT TIME: _____

_____

_____

_____

_____

_____

_____

# PRIMARY FERMENTATION

Date: _____ / _____ / _____          #_____

Ingredients:_____

_____

_____

_____

_____

_____

_____

Yeast:_____

Gallons of Must:_____

Notes:_____

_____

_____

_____

_____

Name:_____

Spc.Grv. Before Correction:_____

Sugar Added:_____

Spc.Grv. After Correction:_____

pH Before Correction:_____

pH After Correction:_____

TA Before:_____

TA Correction:_____

TA After:_____

Totas SO2:_____

# SECONDARY FERMENTATION

| Date | Racked | Spc.Grv. | pH | SO2 | Gallons | Additions |
|------|--------|----------|-----|-----|---------|-----------|
| __ / __ / __ | ☐ | _____ | _____ | _____ | _____ | _____ |

Notes:_____

_____

| __ / __ / __ | ☐ | _____ | _____ | _____ | _____ | _____ |

Notes:_____

_____

| __ / __ / __ | ☐ | _____ | _____ | _____ | _____ | _____ |

Notes:_____

_____

| __ / __ / __ | ☐ | _____ | _____ | _____ | _____ | _____ |

Notes:_____

_____

| __ / __ / __ | ☐ | _____ | _____ | _____ | _____ | _____ |

Notes:_____

_____

| __ / __ / __ | ☐ | _____ | _____ | _____ | _____ | _____ |

Notes:_____

_____

# BOTTLING: _____ / _____ / _____

Spc.Grv. Before Sweetening:_____

Sugar Added:_____

Final pH:_____

Final SO2:_____

Final TA:_____

# of Bottles:_____

% Alcohol By Volume:_____

Notes:_____

_____

_____

_____

_____

_____

_____

_____

_____

_____

ATTACH
LABEL
HERE

# TASTING

Color:_____

Body / Flavor:_____

Finish:_____

Tasting Notes:_____

_____

_____

_____

_____

_____

_____

_____

# NOTES FOR NEXT TIME: _____

_____

_____

_____

_____

_____

_____

# PRIMARY FERMENTATION

Date: _____ / _____ / _____      #_____

Name:_____

Ingredients:_____

Spc.Grv. Before Correction:_____

_____

Sugar Added:_____

_____

Spc.Grv. After Correction:_____

_____

pH Before Correction:_____

_____

pH After Correction:_____

_____

TA Before:_____

_____

TA Correction:_____

_____

TA After:_____

Yeast:_____

Gallons of Must:_____

Totas SO2:_____

Notes:_____

_____

_____

_____

_____

# SECONDARY FERMENTATION

| Date | Racked | Spc.Grv. | pH | SO2 | Gallons | Additions |
|------|--------|----------|-----|-----|---------|-----------|
| ___ / ___ / ___ | ☐ | _____ | _____ | _____ | _____ | _____ |

Notes:_____

_____

| ___ / ___ / ___ | ☐ | _____ | _____ | _____ | _____ | _____ |

Notes:_____

_____

| ___ / ___ / ___ | ☐ | _____ | _____ | _____ | _____ | _____ |

Notes:_____

_____

| ___ / ___ / ___ | ☐ | _____ | _____ | _____ | _____ | _____ |

Notes:_____

_____

| ___ / ___ / ___ | ☐ | _____ | _____ | _____ | _____ | _____ |

Notes:_____

_____

| ___ / ___ / ___ | ☐ | _____ | _____ | _____ | _____ | _____ |

Notes:_____

_____

# BOTTLING: _____ / _____ / _____

Spc.Grv. Before Sweetening:_____

Sugar Added:_____

Final pH:_____

Final SO2:_____

Final TA:_____

# of Bottles:_____

% Alcohol By Volume:_____

Notes:_____

_____

_____

_____

_____

_____

_____

_____

_____

ATTACH
LABEL
HERE

# TASTING

Color:_____

Body / Flavor:_____

Finish:_____

Tasting Notes:_____

_____

_____

_____

_____

_____

_____

_____

# NOTES FOR NEXT TIME: _____

_____

_____

_____

_____

_____

_____

# PRIMARY FERMENTATION

Date: _____ / _____ / _____  #_____

Name:_____

Ingredients:_____

Spc.Grv. Before Correction:_____

_____

Sugar Added:_____

_____

Spc.Grv. After Correction:_____

_____

pH Before Correction:_____

_____

pH After Correction:_____

_____

TA Before:_____

_____

TA Correction:_____

Yeast:_____

TA After:_____

Gallons of Must:_____

Totas SO2:_____

Notes:_____

_____

_____

_____

# SECONDARY FERMENTATION

| Date | Racked | Spc.Grv. | pH | SO2 | Gallons | Additions |
|------|--------|----------|-----|-----|---------|-----------|
| __ / __ / __ | ☐ | _____ | _____ | _____ | _____ | _____ |

Notes:_____

_____

| __ / __ / __ | ☐ | _____ | _____ | _____ | _____ | _____ |

Notes:_____

_____

| __ / __ / __ | ☐ | _____ | _____ | _____ | _____ | _____ |

Notes:_____

_____

| __ / __ / __ | ☐ | _____ | _____ | _____ | _____ | _____ |

Notes:_____

_____

| __ / __ / __ | ☐ | _____ | _____ | _____ | _____ | _____ |

Notes:_____

_____

| __ / __ / __ | ☐ | _____ | _____ | _____ | _____ | _____ |

Notes:_____

_____

# BOTTLING: _____ / _____ / _____

Spc.Grv. Before Sweetening:_____

Sugar Added:_____

Final pH:_____

Final SO2:_____

Final TA:_____

# of Bottles:_____

% Alcohol By Volume:_____

Notes:_____

_____

_____

_____

_____

_____

_____

_____

_____

ATTACH
LABEL
HERE

# TASTING

Color:_____

Body / Flavor:_____

Finish:_____

Tasting Notes:_____

_____

_____

_____

_____

_____

_____

_____

# NOTES FOR NEXT TIME: _____

_____

_____

_____

_____

_____

_____

# PRIMARY FERMENTATION

Date: _____ / _____ / _____     #_____

Name:_____

Ingredients:_____

_____

Spc.Grv. Before Correction:_____

_____

Sugar Added:_____

_____

Spc.Grv. After Correction:_____

_____

pH Before Correction:_____

_____

pH After Correction:_____

_____

TA Before:_____

_____

TA Correction:_____

Yeast:_____

TA After:_____

Gallons of Must:_____

Totas SO2:_____

Notes:_____

_____

_____

_____

# SECONDARY FERMENTATION

| Date | Racked | Spc.Grv. | pH | SO2 | Gallons | Additions |
|------|--------|----------|-----|-----|---------|-----------|
| __ / __ / __ | ☐ | _____ | _____ | _____ | _____ | _____ |
| Notes:_____ | | | | | | |
| __ / __ / __ | ☐ | _____ | _____ | _____ | _____ | _____ |
| Notes:_____ | | | | | | |
| __ / __ / __ | ☐ | _____ | _____ | _____ | _____ | _____ |
| Notes:_____ | | | | | | |
| __ / __ / __ | ☐ | _____ | _____ | _____ | _____ | _____ |
| Notes:_____ | | | | | | |
| __ / __ / __ | ☐ | _____ | _____ | _____ | _____ | _____ |
| Notes:_____ | | | | | | |
| __ / __ / __ | ☐ | _____ | _____ | _____ | _____ | _____ |
| Notes:_____ | | | | | | |

# BOTTLING: _____ / _____ / _____

Spc.Grv. Before Sweetening:_____

Sugar Added:_____

Final pH:_____

Final SO2:_____

Final TA:_____

# of Bottles:_____

% Alcohol By Volume:_____

Notes:_____

_____

_____

_____

_____

_____

_____

_____

ATTACH
LABEL
HERE

_____

_____

# TASTING

Color:_____

Body / Flavor:_____

Finish:_____

Tasting Notes:_____

_____

_____

_____

_____

_____

_____

_____

_____

# NOTES FOR NEXT TIME: _____

_____

_____

_____

_____

_____

_____

# PRIMARY FERMENTATION

Date: _____ / _____ / _____        #_____        Name:_____

Ingredients:_____        Spc.Grv. Before Correction:_____

_____        Sugar Added:_____

_____        Spc.Grv. After Correction:_____

_____        pH Before Correction:_____

_____        pH After Correction:_____

_____        TA Before:_____

_____        TA Correction:_____

Yeast:_____        TA After:_____

Gallons of Must:_____        Totas SO2:_____

Notes:_____

_____

_____

_____

# SECONDARY FERMENTATION

| Date | Racked | Spc.Grv. | pH | SO2 | Gallons | Additions |
|------|--------|----------|-----|-----|---------|-----------|
| __ / __ / __ | ☐ | _____ | _____ | _____ | _____ | _____ |

Notes:_____

_____

| __ / __ / __ | ☐ | _____ | _____ | _____ | _____ | _____ |

Notes:_____

_____

| __ / __ / __ | ☐ | _____ | _____ | _____ | _____ | _____ |

Notes:_____

_____

| __ / __ / __ | ☐ | _____ | _____ | _____ | _____ | _____ |

Notes:_____

_____

| __ / __ / __ | ☐ | _____ | _____ | _____ | _____ | _____ |

Notes:_____

_____

| __ / __ / __ | ☐ | _____ | _____ | _____ | _____ | _____ |

Notes:_____

_____

# BOTTLING: _____ / _____ / _____

Spc.Grv. Before Sweetening:_____

Sugar Added:_____

Final pH:_____

Final SO2:_____

Final TA:_____

# of Bottles:_____

% Alcohol By Volume:_____

Notes:_____

_____

_____

_____

_____

_____

_____

_____

_____

Attach
Label
Here

# TASTING

Color:_____

Body / Flavor:_____

Finish:_____

Tasting Notes:_____

_____

_____

_____

_____

_____

_____

_____

_____

# NOTES FOR NEXT TIME: _____

_____

_____

_____

_____

_____

_____

# PRIMARY FERMENTATION

Date: _____ / _____ / _____     #_____

Ingredients:_____

_____

_____

_____

_____

_____

_____

Yeast:_____

Gallons of Must:_____

Notes:_____

_____

_____

_____

_____

Name:_____

Spc.Grv. Before Correction:_____

Sugar Added:_____

Spc.Grv. After Correction:_____

pH Before Correction:_____

pH After Correction:_____

TA Before:_____

TA Correction:_____

TA After:_____

Totas SO2:_____

# SECONDARY FERMENTATION

| Date | Racked | Spc.Grv. | pH | SO2 | Gallons | Additions |
|------|--------|----------|-----|-----|---------|-----------|
| ___/___/___ | ☐ | _____ | _____ | _____ | _____ | _____ |

Notes:_____

_____

| ___/___/___ | ☐ | _____ | _____ | _____ | _____ | _____ |

Notes:_____

_____

| ___/___/___ | ☐ | _____ | _____ | _____ | _____ | _____ |

Notes:_____

_____

| ___/___/___ | ☐ | _____ | _____ | _____ | _____ | _____ |

Notes:_____

_____

| ___/___/___ | ☐ | _____ | _____ | _____ | _____ | _____ |

Notes:_____

_____

| ___/___/___ | ☐ | _____ | _____ | _____ | _____ | _____ |

Notes:_____

_____

# BOTTLING: _____ / _____ / _____

Spc.Grv. Before Sweetening:_____

Sugar Added:_____

Final pH:_____

Final SO2:_____

Final TA:_____

# of Bottles:_____

% Alcohol By Volume:_____

Notes:_____

_____

_____

_____

_____

_____

_____

_____

_____

ATTACH LABEL HERE

# TASTING

Color:_____

Body / Flavor:_____

Finish:_____

Tasting Notes:_____

_____

_____

_____

_____

_____

_____

_____

# NOTES FOR NEXT TIME: _____

_____

_____

_____

_____

_____

_____

# PRIMARY FERMENTATION

Date: _____ / _____ / _____        #_____

Name:_____

Ingredients:_____

Spc.Grv. Before Correction:_____

_____

Sugar Added:_____

_____

Spc.Grv. After Correction:_____

_____

pH Before Correction:_____

_____

pH After Correction:_____

_____

TA Before:_____

_____

TA Correction:_____

Yeast:_____

TA After:_____

Gallons of Must:_____

Totas SO2:_____

Notes:_____

_____

_____

_____

# SECONDARY FERMENTATION

| Date | Racked | Spc.Grv. | pH | SO2 | Gallons | Additions |
|------|--------|----------|-----|-----|---------|-----------|
| ___ / ___ / ___ | ☐ | _____ | _____ | _____ | _____ | _____ |
| Notes: | | | | | | |
| ___ / ___ / ___ | ☐ | _____ | _____ | _____ | _____ | _____ |
| Notes: | | | | | | |
| ___ / ___ / ___ | ☐ | _____ | _____ | _____ | _____ | _____ |
| Notes: | | | | | | |
| ___ / ___ / ___ | ☐ | _____ | _____ | _____ | _____ | _____ |
| Notes: | | | | | | |
| ___ / ___ / ___ | ☐ | _____ | _____ | _____ | _____ | _____ |
| Notes: | | | | | | |
| ___ / ___ / ___ | ☐ | _____ | _____ | _____ | _____ | _____ |
| Notes: | | | | | | |

# BOTTLING: _____ / _____ / _____

Spc.Grv. Before Sweetening:_____

Sugar Added:_____

Final pH:_____

Final SO2:_____

Final TA:_____

# of Bottles:_____

% Alcohol By Volume:_____


Notes:_____

_____

_____

_____

_____

_____

_____

_____

_____

Attach Label Here

# TASTING

Color:_____

Body / Flavor:_____

Finish:_____

Tasting Notes:_____

_____

_____

_____

_____

_____

_____

_____

# NOTES FOR NEXT TIME: _____

_____

_____

_____

_____

_____

_____

# PRIMARY FERMENTATION

Date: _____ / _____ / _____     #_____

Name:_____

Ingredients:_____

Spc.Grv. Before Correction:_____

_____

Sugar Added:_____

_____

Spc.Grv. After Correction:_____

_____

pH Before Correction:_____

_____

pH After Correction:_____

_____

TA Before:_____

_____

TA Correction:_____

Yeast:_____

TA After:_____

Gallons of Must:_____

Totas SO2:_____

Notes:_____

_____

_____

_____

# SECONDARY FERMENTATION

| Date | Racked | Spc.Grv. | pH | SO2 | Gallons | Additions |
|------|--------|----------|-----|-----|---------|-----------|
| ___/___/___ | ☐ | _____ | _____ | _____ | _____ | _____ |

Notes:_____

_____

| ___/___/___ | ☐ | _____ | _____ | _____ | _____ | _____ |

Notes:_____

_____

| ___/___/___ | ☐ | _____ | _____ | _____ | _____ | _____ |

Notes:_____

_____

| ___/___/___ | ☐ | _____ | _____ | _____ | _____ | _____ |

Notes:_____

_____

| ___/___/___ | ☐ | _____ | _____ | _____ | _____ | _____ |

Notes:_____

_____

| ___/___/___ | ☐ | _____ | _____ | _____ | _____ | _____ |

Notes:_____

_____

# BOTTLING: _____ / _____ / _____

Spc.Grv. Before Sweetening:_____

Sugar Added:_____

Final pH:_____

Final SO2:_____

Final TA:_____

# of Bottles:_____

% Alcohol By Volume:_____

Notes:_____

_____

_____

_____

_____

_____

_____

_____

_____

ATTACH
LABEL
HERE

# TASTING

Color:_____

Body / Flavor:_____

Finish:_____

Tasting Notes:_____

_____

_____

_____

_____

_____

_____

_____

# NOTES FOR NEXT TIME: _____

_____

_____

_____

_____

_____

_____

# PRIMARY FERMENTATION

Date: _____ / _____ / _____          #_____

Name:_____

Ingredients:_____

_____

_____

_____

_____

_____

_____

Yeast:_____

Gallons of Must:_____

Spc.Grv. Before Correction:_____

Sugar Added:_____

Spc.Grv. After Correction:_____

pH Before Correction:_____

pH After Correction:_____

TA Before:_____

TA Correction:_____

TA After:_____

Totas SO2:_____

Notes:_____

_____

_____

_____

_____

# SECONDARY FERMENTATION

| Date | Racked | Spc.Grv. | pH | SO2 | Gallons | Additions |
|------|--------|----------|-----|-----|---------|-----------|
| __ / __ / __ | ☐ | _____ | _____ | _____ | _____ | _____ |

Notes:_____

_____

| __ / __ / __ | ☐ | _____ | _____ | _____ | _____ | _____ |

Notes:_____

_____

| __ / __ / __ | ☐ | _____ | _____ | _____ | _____ | _____ |

Notes:_____

_____

| __ / __ / __ | ☐ | _____ | _____ | _____ | _____ | _____ |

Notes:_____

_____

| __ / __ / __ | ☐ | _____ | _____ | _____ | _____ | _____ |

Notes:_____

_____

| __ / __ / __ | ☐ | _____ | _____ | _____ | _____ | _____ |

Notes:_____

_____

# BOTTLING: _____ / _____ / _____

Spc.Grv. Before Sweetening:_____

Sugar Added:_____

Final pH:_____

Final SO2:_____

Final TA:_____

# of Bottles:_____

% Alcohol By Volume:_____

Notes:_____

_____

_____

_____

_____

_____

_____

ATTACH
LABEL
HERE

_____

_____

# TASTING

Color:_____

Body / Flavor:_____

Finish:_____

Tasting Notes:_____

_____

_____

_____

_____

_____

_____

_____

# NOTES FOR NEXT TIME: _____

_____

_____

_____

_____

_____

_____

# PRIMARY FERMENTATION

Date: _____ / _____ / _____     #_____

Ingredients:_____

_____

_____

_____

_____

_____

_____

Yeast:_____

Gallons of Must:_____

Notes:_____

_____

_____

_____

_____

Name:_____

Spc.Grv. Before Correction:_____

Sugar Added:_____

Spc.Grv. After Correction:_____

pH Before Correction:_____

pH After Correction:_____

TA Before:_____

TA Correction:_____

TA After:_____

Totas SO2:_____

# SECONDARY FERMENTATION

| Date | Racked | Spc.Grv. | pH | SO2 | Gallons | Additions |
|------|--------|----------|-----|-----|---------|-----------|
| ___ / ___ / ___ | ☐ | _____ | _____ | _____ | _____ | _____ |

Notes:_____

_____

| ___ / ___ / ___ | ☐ | _____ | _____ | _____ | _____ | _____ |

Notes:_____

_____

| ___ / ___ / ___ | ☐ | _____ | _____ | _____ | _____ | _____ |

Notes:_____

_____

| ___ / ___ / ___ | ☐ | _____ | _____ | _____ | _____ | _____ |

Notes:_____

_____

| ___ / ___ / ___ | ☐ | _____ | _____ | _____ | _____ | _____ |

Notes:_____

_____

| ___ / ___ / ___ | ☐ | _____ | _____ | _____ | _____ | _____ |

Notes:_____

_____

# BOTTLING: _____ /_____ /_____

Spc.Grv. Before Sweetening:_____

Sugar Added:_____

Final pH:_____

Final SO2:_____

Final TA:_____

# of Bottles:_____

% Alcohol By Volume:_____


Notes:_____

_____

_____

_____

_____

_____

_____

_____

_____

Attach Label Here

# TASTING

Color:_____

Body / Flavor:_____

Finish:_____

Tasting Notes:_____

_____

_____

_____

_____

_____

_____

_____

# NOTES FOR NEXT TIME: _____

_____

_____

_____

_____

_____

_____

## TO STABALIZE WINE (Per Gallon)

1/2 tsp Potassium Sorbate

1 Crushed Campden Tablet

## YEAST STARTER RECIPE

Ingredients: (For a 5 gallon batch of wine)

3 ounces frozen 100% orange juice concentrate

24 ounces water

3/4 cup sugar

2 rounded teaspoons of ordinary yeast nutrient

1 packet of yeast (Lalvin K1-V1116 or EC-1118 works very well.)

Heat the water, frozen orange juice, and sugar in a 2-quart sauce pan. When the mix boils, remove it from the heat, add the nutrient, and cover the sauce pan. Cool the mix to room temperature (an ice bath may be used). Transfer the starter mix to a sterilized 1-gallon jug (or an erlynmeyer flask). Add the yeast culture and attach an air lock. After 2 to 6 hours when the solution is in an active ferment (much $CO_2$ is expelled through the air lock when swiveled) it is ready to add to the must.

Printed with permission and special thanks to:

The House of Homebrew at houseofhomebrew.com

## YEAST REHYDRATION

1. Allow yeast to warm to room temperature

2. Dissolve yeast in 2oz warm (104-109F) water.

3. Let sit for 15 minutes (DO NOT STIR)

4. Stir well.

5. Add to must.

## YOUR NOTES

## YOUR NOTES

# YOUR NOTES

# YOUR NOTES

# YOUR NOTES

# YOUR NOTES

## CARBOY TAG

Name:_____ #_____
Start Date: _____ / _____ / _____
Next Racking Date:        Spc.Grv.        Note
_____ / _____ / _____
_____ / _____ / _____
_____ / _____ / _____
_____ / _____ / _____
_____ / _____ / _____
_____ / _____ / _____
_____ / _____ / _____

## CARBOY TAG

Name:_____ #_____
Start Date: _____ / _____ / _____
Next Racking Date:        Spc.Grv.        Note
_____ / _____ / _____
_____ / _____ / _____
_____ / _____ / _____
_____ / _____ / _____
_____ / _____ / _____
_____ / _____ / _____
_____ / _____ / _____

## CARBOY TAG

Name:_____ #_____
Start Date: _____ / _____ / _____
Next Racking Date:        Spc.Grv.        Note
_____ / _____ / _____
_____ / _____ / _____
_____ / _____ / _____
_____ / _____ / _____
_____ / _____ / _____
_____ / _____ / _____
_____ / _____ / _____

## CARBOY TAG

Name:_____ #_____
Start Date: _____ / _____ / _____
Next Racking Date:        Spc.Grv.        Note
_____ / _____ / _____
_____ / _____ / _____
_____ / _____ / _____
_____ / _____ / _____
_____ / _____ / _____
_____ / _____ / _____
_____ / _____ / _____

## CARBOY TAG

Name:_____ #_____
Start Date: _____ / _____ / _____
Next Racking Date:        Spc.Grv.        Note
_____ / _____ / _____
_____ / _____ / _____
_____ / _____ / _____
_____ / _____ / _____
_____ / _____ / _____
_____ / _____ / _____
_____ / _____ / _____

## CARBOY TAG

Name:_____ #_____
Start Date: _____ / _____ / _____
Next Racking Date:        Spc.Grv.        Note
_____ / _____ / _____
_____ / _____ / _____
_____ / _____ / _____
_____ / _____ / _____
_____ / _____ / _____
_____ / _____ / _____
_____ / _____ / _____

## CARBOY TAG

Name:_____ #_____
Start Date: _____ / _____ / _____
Next Racking Date:          Spc.Grv.          Note
_____ / _____ / _____
_____ / _____ / _____
_____ / _____ / _____
_____ / _____ / _____
_____ / _____ / _____
_____ / _____ / _____
_____ / _____ / _____

## CARBOY TAG

Name:_____ #_____
Start Date: _____ / _____ / _____
Next Racking Date:          Spc.Grv.          Note
_____ / _____ / _____
_____ / _____ / _____
_____ / _____ / _____
_____ / _____ / _____
_____ / _____ / _____
_____ / _____ / _____
_____ / _____ / _____

## CARBOY TAG

Name:_____ #_____
Start Date: _____ / _____ / _____
Next Racking Date:          Spc.Grv.          Note
_____ / _____ / _____
_____ / _____ / _____
_____ / _____ / _____
_____ / _____ / _____
_____ / _____ / _____
_____ / _____ / _____
_____ / _____ / _____

## CARBOY TAG

Name:_____ #_____
Start Date: _____ / _____ / _____
Next Racking Date:          Spc.Grv.          Note
_____ / _____ / _____
_____ / _____ / _____
_____ / _____ / _____
_____ / _____ / _____
_____ / _____ / _____
_____ / _____ / _____
_____ / _____ / _____

## CARBOY TAG

Name:_____ #_____
Start Date: _____ / _____ / _____
Next Racking Date:          Spc.Grv.          Note
_____ / _____ / _____
_____ / _____ / _____
_____ / _____ / _____
_____ / _____ / _____
_____ / _____ / _____
_____ / _____ / _____
_____ / _____ / _____

## CARBOY TAG

Name:_____ #_____
Start Date: _____ / _____ / _____
Next Racking Date:          Spc.Grv.          Note
_____ / _____ / _____
_____ / _____ / _____
_____ / _____ / _____
_____ / _____ / _____
_____ / _____ / _____
_____ / _____ / _____
_____ / _____ / _____

## CARBOY TAG

Name:_____ #_____

Start Date: _____ / _____ / _____

Next Racking Date:          Spc.Grv.          Note

_____ / _____ / _____

_____ / _____ / _____

_____ / _____ / _____

_____ / _____ / _____

_____ / _____ / _____

_____ / _____ / _____

_____ / _____ / _____


## CARBOY TAG

Name:_____ #_____

Start Date: _____ / _____ / _____

Next Racking Date:          Spc.Grv.          Note

_____ / _____ / _____

_____ / _____ / _____

_____ / _____ / _____

_____ / _____ / _____

_____ / _____ / _____

_____ / _____ / _____

_____ / _____ / _____


## CARBOY TAG

Name:_____ #_____

Start Date: _____ / _____ / _____

Next Racking Date:          Spc.Grv.          Note

_____ / _____ / _____

_____ / _____ / _____

_____ / _____ / _____

_____ / _____ / _____

_____ / _____ / _____

_____ / _____ / _____

_____ / _____ / _____


## CARBOY TAG

Name:_____ #_____

Start Date: _____ / _____ / _____

Next Racking Date:          Spc.Grv.          Note

_____ / _____ / _____

_____ / _____ / _____

_____ / _____ / _____

_____ / _____ / _____

_____ / _____ / _____

_____ / _____ / _____

_____ / _____ / _____


## CARBOY TAG

Name:_____ #_____

Start Date: _____ / _____ / _____

Next Racking Date:          Spc.Grv.          Note

_____ / _____ / _____

_____ / _____ / _____

_____ / _____ / _____

_____ / _____ / _____

_____ / _____ / _____

_____ / _____ / _____

_____ / _____ / _____


## CARBOY TAG

Name:_____ #_____

Start Date: _____ / _____ / _____

Next Racking Date:          Spc.Grv.          Note

_____ / _____ / _____

_____ / _____ / _____

_____ / _____ / _____

_____ / _____ / _____

_____ / _____ / _____

_____ / _____ / _____

_____ / _____ / _____

## CARBOY TAG

Name:_____ #_____

Start Date: _____ / _____ / _____

Next Racking Date:          Spc.Grv.          Note
_____ / _____ / _____
_____ / _____ / _____
_____ / _____ / _____
_____ / _____ / _____
_____ / _____ / _____
_____ / _____ / _____
_____ / _____ / _____

## CARBOY TAG

Name:_____ #_____

Start Date: _____ / _____ / _____

Next Racking Date:          Spc.Grv.          Note
_____ / _____ / _____
_____ / _____ / _____
_____ / _____ / _____
_____ / _____ / _____
_____ / _____ / _____
_____ / _____ / _____
_____ / _____ / _____

## CARBOY TAG

Name:_____ #_____

Start Date: _____ / _____ / _____

Next Racking Date:          Spc.Grv.          Note
_____ / _____ / _____
_____ / _____ / _____
_____ / _____ / _____
_____ / _____ / _____
_____ / _____ / _____
_____ / _____ / _____
_____ / _____ / _____

## CARBOY TAG

Name:_____ #_____

Start Date: _____ / _____ / _____

Next Racking Date:          Spc.Grv.          Note
_____ / _____ / _____
_____ / _____ / _____
_____ / _____ / _____
_____ / _____ / _____
_____ / _____ / _____
_____ / _____ / _____
_____ / _____ / _____

## CARBOY TAG

Name:_____ #_____

Start Date: _____ / _____ / _____

Next Racking Date:          Spc.Grv.          Note
_____ / _____ / _____
_____ / _____ / _____
_____ / _____ / _____
_____ / _____ / _____
_____ / _____ / _____
_____ / _____ / _____
_____ / _____ / _____

## CARBOY TAG

Name:_____ #_____

Start Date: _____ / _____ / _____

Next Racking Date:          Spc.Grv.          Note
_____ / _____ / _____
_____ / _____ / _____
_____ / _____ / _____
_____ / _____ / _____
_____ / _____ / _____
_____ / _____ / _____
_____ / _____ / _____

## CARBOY TAG

Name:_____ #_____
Start Date: _____ / _____ / _____
Next Racking Date:        Spc.Grv.        Note
_____ / _____ / _____
_____ / _____ / _____
_____ / _____ / _____
_____ / _____ / _____
_____ / _____ / _____
_____ / _____ / _____
_____ / _____ / _____

## CARBOY TAG

Name:_____ #_____
Start Date: _____ / _____ / _____
Next Racking Date:        Spc.Grv.        Note
_____ / _____ / _____
_____ / _____ / _____
_____ / _____ / _____
_____ / _____ / _____
_____ / _____ / _____
_____ / _____ / _____
_____ / _____ / _____

## CARBOY TAG

Name:_____ #_____
Start Date: _____ / _____ / _____
Next Racking Date:        Spc.Grv.        Note
_____ / _____ / _____
_____ / _____ / _____
_____ / _____ / _____
_____ / _____ / _____
_____ / _____ / _____
_____ / _____ / _____
_____ / _____ / _____

## CARBOY TAG

Name:_____ #_____
Start Date: _____ / _____ / _____
Next Racking Date:        Spc.Grv.        Note
_____ / _____ / _____
_____ / _____ / _____
_____ / _____ / _____
_____ / _____ / _____
_____ / _____ / _____
_____ / _____ / _____
_____ / _____ / _____

## CARBOY TAG

Name:_____ #_____
Start Date: _____ / _____ / _____
Next Racking Date:        Spc.Grv.        Note
_____ / _____ / _____
_____ / _____ / _____
_____ / _____ / _____
_____ / _____ / _____
_____ / _____ / _____
_____ / _____ / _____
_____ / _____ / _____

## CARBOY TAG

Name:_____ #_____
Start Date: _____ / _____ / _____
Next Racking Date:        Spc.Grv.        Note
_____ / _____ / _____
_____ / _____ / _____
_____ / _____ / _____
_____ / _____ / _____
_____ / _____ / _____
_____ / _____ / _____
_____ / _____ / _____

## CARBOY TAG

Name:_____ #_____

Start Date: _____ / _____ / _____

Next Racking Date:        Spc.Grv.        Note

_____ / _____ / _____

_____ / _____ / _____

_____ / _____ / _____

_____ / _____ / _____

_____ / _____ / _____

_____ / _____ / _____

_____ / _____ / _____

## CARBOY TAG

Name:_____ #_____

Start Date: _____ / _____ / _____

Next Racking Date:        Spc.Grv.        Note

_____ / _____ / _____

_____ / _____ / _____

_____ / _____ / _____

_____ / _____ / _____

_____ / _____ / _____

_____ / _____ / _____

_____ / _____ / _____

## CARBOY TAG

Name:_____ #_____

Start Date: _____ / _____ / _____

Next Racking Date:        Spc.Grv.        Note

_____ / _____ / _____

_____ / _____ / _____

_____ / _____ / _____

_____ / _____ / _____

_____ / _____ / _____

_____ / _____ / _____

_____ / _____ / _____

## CARBOY TAG

Name:_____ #_____

Start Date: _____ / _____ / _____

Next Racking Date:        Spc.Grv.        Note

_____ / _____ / _____

_____ / _____ / _____

_____ / _____ / _____

_____ / _____ / _____

_____ / _____ / _____

_____ / _____ / _____

_____ / _____ / _____

## CARBOY TAG

Name:_____ #_____

Start Date: _____ / _____ / _____

Next Racking Date:        Spc.Grv.        Note

_____ / _____ / _____

_____ / _____ / _____

_____ / _____ / _____

_____ / _____ / _____

_____ / _____ / _____

_____ / _____ / _____

_____ / _____ / _____

## CARBOY TAG

Name:_____ #_____

Start Date: _____ / _____ / _____

Next Racking Date:        Spc.Grv.        Note

_____ / _____ / _____

_____ / _____ / _____

_____ / _____ / _____

_____ / _____ / _____

_____ / _____ / _____

_____ / _____ / _____

_____ / _____ / _____

## CARBOY TAG

Name:_____ #_____
Start Date: _____ / _____ / _____
Next Racking Date:        Spc.Grv.        Note
_____ / _____ / _____
_____ / _____ / _____
_____ / _____ / _____
_____ / _____ / _____
_____ / _____ / _____
_____ / _____ / _____
_____ / _____ / _____

## CARBOY TAG

Name:_____ #_____
Start Date: _____ / _____ / _____
Next Racking Date:        Spc.Grv.        Note
_____ / _____ / _____
_____ / _____ / _____
_____ / _____ / _____
_____ / _____ / _____
_____ / _____ / _____
_____ / _____ / _____
_____ / _____ / _____

## CARBOY TAG

Name:_____ #_____
Start Date: _____ / _____ / _____
Next Racking Date:        Spc.Grv.        Note
_____ / _____ / _____
_____ / _____ / _____
_____ / _____ / _____
_____ / _____ / _____
_____ / _____ / _____
_____ / _____ / _____
_____ / _____ / _____

## CARBOY TAG

Name:_____ #_____
Start Date: _____ / _____ / _____
Next Racking Date:        Spc.Grv.        Note
_____ / _____ / _____
_____ / _____ / _____
_____ / _____ / _____
_____ / _____ / _____
_____ / _____ / _____
_____ / _____ / _____
_____ / _____ / _____

## CARBOY TAG

Name:_____ #_____
Start Date: _____ / _____ / _____
Next Racking Date:        Spc.Grv.        Note
_____ / _____ / _____
_____ / _____ / _____
_____ / _____ / _____
_____ / _____ / _____
_____ / _____ / _____
_____ / _____ / _____
_____ / _____ / _____

## CARBOY TAG

Name:_____ #_____
Start Date: _____ / _____ / _____
Next Racking Date:        Spc.Grv.        Note
_____ / _____ / _____
_____ / _____ / _____
_____ / _____ / _____
_____ / _____ / _____
_____ / _____ / _____
_____ / _____ / _____
_____ / _____ / _____

## CARBOY TAG

Name:_____ #_____
Start Date: _____ / _____ / _____
Next Racking Date:        Spc.Grv.        Note
_____ / _____ / _____
_____ / _____ / _____
_____ / _____ / _____
_____ / _____ / _____
_____ / _____ / _____
_____ / _____ / _____
_____ / _____ / _____

## CARBOY TAG

Name:_____ #_____
Start Date: _____ / _____ / _____
Next Racking Date:        Spc.Grv.        Note
_____ / _____ / _____
_____ / _____ / _____
_____ / _____ / _____
_____ / _____ / _____
_____ / _____ / _____
_____ / _____ / _____
_____ / _____ / _____

## CARBOY TAG

Name:_____ #_____
Start Date: _____ / _____ / _____
Next Racking Date:        Spc.Grv.        Note
_____ / _____ / _____
_____ / _____ / _____
_____ / _____ / _____
_____ / _____ / _____
_____ / _____ / _____
_____ / _____ / _____
_____ / _____ / _____

## CARBOY TAG

Name:_____ #_____
Start Date: _____ / _____ / _____
Next Racking Date:        Spc.Grv.        Note
_____ / _____ / _____
_____ / _____ / _____
_____ / _____ / _____
_____ / _____ / _____
_____ / _____ / _____
_____ / _____ / _____
_____ / _____ / _____

## CARBOY TAG

Name:_____ #_____
Start Date: _____ / _____ / _____
Next Racking Date:        Spc.Grv.        Note
_____ / _____ / _____
_____ / _____ / _____
_____ / _____ / _____
_____ / _____ / _____
_____ / _____ / _____
_____ / _____ / _____
_____ / _____ / _____

## CARBOY TAG

Name:_____ #_____
Start Date: _____ / _____ / _____
Next Racking Date:        Spc.Grv.        Note
_____ / _____ / _____
_____ / _____ / _____
_____ / _____ / _____
_____ / _____ / _____
_____ / _____ / _____
_____ / _____ / _____
_____ / _____ / _____

## CARBOY TAG

Name:_____ #_____

Start Date: _____ / _____ / _____

Next Racking Date:    Spc.Grv.    Note

_____ / _____ / _____

_____ / _____ / _____

_____ / _____ / _____

_____ / _____ / _____

_____ / _____ / _____

_____ / _____ / _____

_____ / _____ / _____

## CARBOY TAG

Name:_____ #_____

Start Date: _____ / _____ / _____

Next Racking Date:    Spc.Grv.    Note

_____ / _____ / _____

_____ / _____ / _____

_____ / _____ / _____

_____ / _____ / _____

_____ / _____ / _____

_____ / _____ / _____

_____ / _____ / _____

## CARBOY TAG

Name:_____ #_____

Start Date: _____ / _____ / _____

Next Racking Date:    Spc.Grv.    Note

_____ / _____ / _____

_____ / _____ / _____

_____ / _____ / _____

_____ / _____ / _____

_____ / _____ / _____

_____ / _____ / _____

_____ / _____ / _____

## CARBOY TAG

Name:_____ #_____

Start Date: _____ / _____ / _____

Next Racking Date:    Spc.Grv.    Note

_____ / _____ / _____

_____ / _____ / _____

_____ / _____ / _____

_____ / _____ / _____

_____ / _____ / _____

_____ / _____ / _____

_____ / _____ / _____

## CARBOY TAG

Name:_____ #_____

Start Date: _____ / _____ / _____

Next Racking Date:    Spc.Grv.    Note

_____ / _____ / _____

_____ / _____ / _____

_____ / _____ / _____

_____ / _____ / _____

_____ / _____ / _____

_____ / _____ / _____

_____ / _____ / _____

## CARBOY TAG

Name:_____ #_____

Start Date: _____ / _____ / _____

Next Racking Date:    Spc.Grv.    Note

_____ / _____ / _____

_____ / _____ / _____

_____ / _____ / _____

_____ / _____ / _____

_____ / _____ / _____

_____ / _____ / _____

_____ / _____ / _____

Made in the USA
San Bernardino, CA
30 November 2016